As a Licensed Marriage and Family Therapist I have read many books on co-dependency but I find Mary Crocker Cook's book, Awakening Hope, to be the most thorough and helpful text on this subject. I especially appreciate the developmental and biological perspectives Mary brings to this work. Mary Crocker Cook is a genius! I'm passing this book on to ALL my co-dependent clients! Melody Beattie, move over! — Beth Elliott-Staggs, LMFT

This book is a brilliant explanation of attachment disorders and quite an easy read if you're interested in human behavior and have some background in psychology or codependency issues. I will read this book again and again to practice recognizing signs in myself and to create long term awareness for myself. — Amazon reviewer

Mary's text is the first to fully capture the attachment issues that are the core of our struggle. Even more powerfully, she connects the adrenal system damage that results from the emotional rollercoaster that drives codependent behavior. While she supports her ideas with solid theory and research, it is her courage in revealing her own personal struggle with these issues that makes the theory come alive. It is unusual for a therapist to be willing to be so candid about her own personal journey, and I felt inspired by it.

— Stacy Smith, LMFT

Awakening Hope

A Developmental, Behavioral, Biological Approach to
Codependency Treatment

~ Revised Edition ~

Mary Crocker Cook, D.Min., LMFT, CADCII

AWAKENING HOPE

© 2011 Mary Crocker Cook

ISBN: 978-1-61170-031-2

Printed in the USA and UK on acid-free paper.

To purchase additional copies of this book go to:
www.rp–author.com/mcook

Third Printing

 Robertson Publishing™
59 North Santa Cruz Avenue
Los Gatos, California 95030 USA
www.RobertsonPublishing.com

Acknowledgement

To Howard Scott Warshaw, my patient editor.

When I wrote the first edition of Awakening Hope I was processing the magnitude of a loss that included the man and business I loved. I wrote to save my sanity, and hoped that what I was learning would assist others to do the same. While I wrote from the heart and from research, I was desperately in need of an editor for the first edition and did not have one.

Howard was kind enough to read my first edition. After seeing my grammatical and sentence structure challenges he thought, "This is great stuff. I need to help her," and graciously offered his editorial services to improve the text. The revised edition of Awakening Hope is the result of his attention to detail and I am profoundly grateful. More significantly Howard came along while I was still in the healing process and working through my own avoidant codependent patterns. The consistent presence of someone willing to help me, expecting nothing from me other than gratitude and an occasional lunch, was confirmation that I was capable of trust when presented with someone trustworthy. I was not "broken" and I was well on my way to remaining fully open-hearted in the face of the temptation to retreat to former avoidant patterns. This reassurance that I am healing is the greater gift.

Thank You, Howard

Mary

A Note From the Editor

I knew Mary as a dynamic and compelling professor/lecturer in my graduate psychology program at JFK University. I took every course she offered because I knew it would be worth it. And it always was! When I heard she was writing a book, my first thought was "How can I help?"

What began as a few tips on creating a marketing video turned into a mutually supportive collaboration and friendship. But the greatest gift by far is that "Awakening Hope" has made me a healthier person and a better clinician. For this I am truly grateful.

I have seen Mary's experience, insight and humor benefit hundreds in the classroom. To help her reach hundreds of thousands is an honor and I am proud to be associated with this work.

"Awakening Hope" will create healthier people and better clinicians.

This is *my* hope.

HSW

First there was me

Then there was Him

Then there was only Him

Then He Left

Then there was no one

CONTENTS

PROLOGUE 1

INTRODUCTION: History of Codependency 5

Working definition of Codependency :
At its heart, Codependency is a set of behaviors developed to manage the anxiety that comes when our primary attachments are formed with people who are inconsistent or unavailable in their response to us. Our anxiety-based responses to life can include over-reactivity, image management, unrealistic beliefs about our limits, and attempts to control the reality of others to the point where we lose our boundaries, self-esteem, and even our own reality. Ultimately, Codependency is a chronic stress disease, which can devastate our immune system and lead to systemic and even life-threatening illness.

PART ONE
At its heart, Codependency is a set of behaviors developed to manage the anxiety that comes when our primary attachments are formed with people who are inconsistent or unavailable in their response to us.

CHAPTER ONE: A Developmental Perspective 13

Attachment Style Quiz
* Review of Attachment Theory

Characteristics of Secure Attachment

Anxious/Ambivalent Attachment and Avoidant/Dismissive Attachment

CHAPTER TWO: Codependency and Attachment Theory 31

* Internal working models and organization of working models into adulthood

* Working models and emotional regulation

CHAPTER THREE: Attachment Patterns Over Time 38

CHAPTER FOUR: Attachment and Addiction and Mental Disorders ..54

CHAPTER FIVE: Family Dynamics That Create Disrupted Attachments..59

PART TWO
Our anxiety-based responses to life can include over-reactivity, image management, unrealistic beliefs about our limits, and attempts to control the reality of others to the point where we lose our boundaries, self-esteem, and even our own reality.

CHAPTER SIX: Codependent Behavioral Characteristics drawn from Attachment Research..75

Anxious/Ambivalent Codependents

- Symptom One: Lack of Attunement with Self

- Symptom Two: Lack of Attunement with others

- Symptom Three: Distrusting the Attachment of others to the Codependent

- Symptom Four: Escalation to protect attachment

Avoidant/Dismissing Codependence

- Symptom Five: Denial of Dependency or Attachment Needs

- Symptom Six: Avoiding Intimacy

- Symptom Seven: Walls Instead of Boundaries

CHAPTER SEVEN: A Few More Notes About Developmental Task Completion oer the Lifespan...109

- Erickson's Developmental Stages

PART THREE
Ultimately, Codependency is a chronic stress disease, which can devastate our immune system and lead to systemic and even life-threatening illness.

CHAPTER EIGHT: Codependency as a Chronic Stress Disorder 120

- Attachment Implications in Developing Chronic Stress Disorders

CHAPTER NINE: Physiology of the Stress Response Connected to Codependency 125

CHAPTER TEN: Stress and the Adrenal Glands....................................133

CHAPTER ELEVEN: Specific Thoughts About Treatment Planning 139

- Symptom One: Lack of Attunement with Self
- Symptom Two: Lack of Attunement with Others
- Symptom Three: Distrusting the Attachment of others to the Codependent
- Symptom Four: Escalation to Protect the Attachment
- Symptom Five: Denial of Dependency or Attachment Needs
- Symptom Six: Avoiding Intimacy
- Symptom Seven: Walls Instead of Boundaries

PART FOUR
Recovery is Possible

CHAPTER TWELVE: Mind-Body Healing for Codependency..............169

- Developmental Issues
- Behavioral Responses
- Biological Consequences

Creating a Treatment Plan

Codependency Relapse Warning Signs

CHAPTER THIRTEEN: Afterword 177

APPENDIX A AINSWORTH'S STRANGE SITUATION....................................183
APPENDIX B NOTE TO THERAPISTS...187
APPENDIX C PSYCHOSOCIAL TASK DEVELOPMENT INVENTORY..............189

FOOTNOTES...207

A Developmental, Behavioral, and Biological Approach to Codependency Treatment

PROLOGUE

Several years ago I met a man. From that moment I believed he was the love of my life. I started a business to be with this man and participated actively in supporting his education, and began and ended every day of my life with the thought of him. He never asked me for any of those things – I volunteered them. After seven years of establishing myself as "indispensable," a woman walked in to our business wearing a tube top. Within three months I had left the business, and him, because I became insane.

Despite his denials of all my accusations, I could not be comforted. I couldn't breathe – I was having at least five panic attacks a day. I couldn't be alone with my thoughts because all I could do was obsess about her and wish me, or her, dead. The pain came in waves and I would find myself literally keening on the floor, where my staff could on occasion hear me wailing because she was in his office behind his locked door. I was suffocating under the weight of the loss because he had been my entire world for such a long time. All he had to do to "fix" the situation was remove her, but he would not do so. The obsessive thoughts that tormented me day and night included, "he chose her over me," and "maybe I hadn't loved him enough," and my gut and chest hurt constantly. I rocked back and forth, doubled over and folded into my abdomen. I now viscerally understand what it means to be "bereft," because I lost both him and me at the same time. Honestly, I wasn't sure I would live through this much pain without permanently losing my mind.

This is not a story about him, or how I was a "victim" because I wasn't. Despite 20 years in the classroom teaching "Codependency and Family Dynamics", as well as 20 years in Al-Anon, "knowledge" did not prevent me from disappearing into him, and the wrenching apart was the hardest and most frightening experience of my life.

In the initial aftermath I chose to "save myself" by deepening my understanding of the role my own attachment disruptions played in laying the foundation of such a profoundly destructive codependent relationship. The breaking of the attachment consumed me to the core so I went back to the early attachment theorists to compose a theory of codependency formation and treatment planning that would address this core level. While this project was born out of desperation and overwhelming grief, I have come to recognize that counseling professionals have been missing important inroads into the permanent healing of what is a developmental, behavioral, and biological disorder. It is my deepest hope that this text will provide guidance and genuine direction in healing for the codependent who suffers and those who are working valiantly to save their lives.

Afraid the pain will
kill me

Afraid it won't

And I'll be left

On the wrong side of
the dirt

HISTORY OF CODEPENDENCY

As I mentioned, I have been teaching a three unit course, Codependency and Family Dynamics, in the San Jose City College Alcohol and Drug Studies Program since 1990. Over twenty years of teaching this material my understanding of the depth and complexity of the disorder has expanded considerably.

My first exposure to the term Codependency was through the addiction field. In the 1970's and early eighties it was often used interchangeably with co-addict or co-alcoholic. The "dependency" referred to the shared effects of addiction experienced by both the alcoholic and their partner. An interchangeable term was "The Enabler," or someone who supported the addict's ability to use by covering up the consequences of the disease.

Early Roots of Codependency

My familiarity with the term grew through the self-help books my clients began to bring into the therapy room in the late 1980's. The term was expanding out past its connection with addiction, and clients would have pages heavily underlined and earmarked – discovering language for the relationship issues and behaviors that had confused them for years.

John Bradshaw and "The Family" series burst onto PBS in the late 1980's, and family systems language long known to marriage and family counselors, and researchers at the MRI Institute in Palo Alto, (Gregory Bateson, Don Jackson, Paul Watzlawick, John Weakland, and Stephanie Brown) was translated into lay language that "made sense" to the viewers. Treatment centers were madly videotaping the series every time it was brought out for the telethon. In fact, I still have the videotaped, grainy copies I reviewed weekly with clients in treatment groups.

When Dr. Murray Bowen developed "The Bowen System" of family therapy, he suggested the whole family as the problem, maintaining that the most distressed and under-functioning person in the family triggered the rest of the family into over-functioning behaviors. The more the family members over-functioned, the more the distressed person under-functioned. Thus, the more the family tried to change the more it stayed the same. Bowen was convinced that the whole family was in need of therapy. Bowen did not use the word "Codependency," but he emphasized that, like a mobile, every member of a diseased family was dependent on his or her other family members.

Family roles and corresponding behaviors, such as the "Hero" and "Mascot" were echoed by addiction authors such as Claudia Black, *It Will Never Happen To Me*. She describes the symptoms she carried as an adult that stemmed from living with an alcoholic father and a co-alcoholic mother. Dr. Black made it clear that her whole alcoholic family was diseased, and that each member was codependent on the alcoholic father.

Pia Mellody, Janet Woititz, Jane Middleton-Moz, and other hands-on clinicians like Dr. Bob Akerman and Sharon Wegscheider Cruse (a protégée of Virginia Satir) were describing the symptoms of the adult children of alcoholic families as "codependent," and fleshed out the "mobile" analogy introduced by Murray Bowen and still used by family therapists. Mellody Beattie's book "Codependent No More" became one of the supportive texts recommended by Codependents Anonymous (founded in 1986 in Phoenix, Arizona) and exploded into the 1990's. Women in counseling groups explored the boundary violations, shame core, and inner child characteristics that marked them Codependent. Anne Wilson Schaef introduced the cultural aspects and influences which both promote and prevent the healing of Codependency.

Attempts to free codependency research and writing from the backwaters of the addiction field culminated with Timmen Cermak's attempt to advocate for inclusion of Codependency diagnostic symptoms as a personality disorder into the Diagnostic and Statistical Manual the diagnostic "Bible" for mental health professionals. Cermak, in *Diagnosing and Treating Codependence*, argued that codependency was on par with other personality disorders. "To be useful though," wrote Cermak, "codependency needs to be unified and described with consistency. It needs a substantive framework and, until this is done, the psychological community will not recognize codependence as a disease."

Predictably, there was a backlash to all this perceived labeling, with concerns such as:

> *Unfortunately, from the mid eighties to the present, the codependency idea has become bastardized, and with each new self-help book the symptoms of codependency mount. It is literally impossible for anyone walking the planet, with a fourth grade English reading capacity, to finish one of these books and not consider the possibility that he or she is a codependent. What began as a term to help spouses of addicts encourage sobriety and not inadvertently make it easy to continue, the codependency movement of the 80s and 90s has thrown the baby out with the bath water: Not only is all caring manifested by the spouse of an alcoholic deemed pathological, but the very act of compromising one's needs to aid a loved one is now deemed symptomatic of a progressive disease processes, a relationship addiction.*
>
> ~ *Robert Westermeyer, Ph.D. author,*
> *WHEN CARING BECOMES A DISEASE*

The term "Codependent" fell out of favor with feminist authors, who observed that codependent descriptions and trait lists pathologized women as well as extended family cultures. Some authors ultimately led the term to be trivialized by declaring 96% of the population to be Codependent!

All of this time I quietly kept teaching my course, working at addiction treatment centers, and providing counseling to individuals and couples. Meanwhile Codependency did not disappear like the "fad" it had been dismissed to be and I deepened my understanding of its origins which lay in the disrupted attachments of early life. I began to include John Bowlby's work with attachment styles in my material and reviewed the anxious and avoidant attachment styles that lay the groundwork for adult symptoms of codependency. Barry and Janae Weinhold's text, "Breaking Free of the Codependency Trap" draws on decades of clinical experience, and correlates the developmental causes of codependency with relationship problems later in life, such as establishing and maintaining boundaries, clinging and dependent behaviors, people pleasing, and difficulty achieving success in the world. However, despite adding this key developmental component, there was more to be understood about this disorder.

In 1998 I first read *"Ghosts in the Nursery: Tracing the Origins of Violence."* The authors, Robin Karr-Morse and Meredith S. Wiley, believe that a predisposition to violent behavior can be learned before birth. A "chemical wash" of toxins such as drugs and alcohol, combined with a mother's stress hormones generated from rage or fear can directly affect the babies brain development. Though Codependency is not a violence issue, I instantly recognized the potential biological issues connecting early trauma and the later reactive styles I observed in myself and my codependent clients. I was further able to comprehend the biology when I came across Tian Dayton's work connecting somatic responses to trauma and codependency. An expert in trauma and psychodrama, Dr. Dayton's book, *Emotional Sobriety: From Relationship Trauma to Resilience and Balance,* explores how the limbic system processes our emotions and governs our mood, appetite, and sleep cycles. Repeated painful experiences in childhood or adulthood (over which we have no control) can over sensitize us to stress and dysregulate our limbic system.

The chronic illnesses developed by Codependents make sense when you follow the results of chronic stress through immune system depletion and wind up with systemic illness. I put together the pieces of what I had seen and experienced over the years and recognized codependency as a destabilizing and physically compromising disorder. The texts I was reading were giving me the language to explain this connection to others. From a three pronged vantage point (developmental, behavioral, and biological) I developed a new direction in addressing the treatment of codependent clients in recovery.

My working definition of Codependency will be:

At its heart, Codependency is a set of behaviors developed to manage the anxiety that comes when our primary attachments are formed with people who are inconsistent or unavailable in their response to us. Our anxiety-based responses to life can include over-reactivity, image management, unrealistic beliefs about our limits, and attempts to control the reality of others to the point where we lose our boundaries, self-esteem, and even our own reality. Ultimately, Codependency is a chronic stress disease, which can devastate our immune system and lead to systemic and even life-threatening illness.

Along the way my intellectual understanding began to deepen into a heart understanding that took my personal journey to new depths. I could see myself more clearly, which was frightening at times, but I also developed greater compassion for my own reactivity based on my early attachment disruption.

Throughout this text, I will explore the three prongs of codependency (developmental, behavioral, and biological) and address approaches to healing at all three levels to assist in more holistic and comprehensive approaches to treatment planning for individuals and for counselors.

My bias is always toward application. Ultimately, material needs to be "useful" in addition to interesting! I will also include vignettes and stories that represent composites of people I have known or treated over time. The only person I will identify specifically in this text will be me. I have included "Soul Collage" cards I made during this period of time both for the "visual" learner and also to illustrate how much healing takes place on an unconscious, non-verbal level. My cards, drawn from my own internal wisdom, comforted me in their reminder that I was making progress. That helped me to see I was healing even when I felt as though I was "regressing" back into the fear and terror of separation.

Thank you for your willingness to take another look at a disorder which not only leads to depression and loss of self, but can damage immune systems and create life-threatening illness.

Awakening Hope

PART ONE

At its heart, Codependency is a set of behaviors developed to manage the anxiety that comes when our primary attachments are formed with people who are inconsistent or unavailable in their response to us.

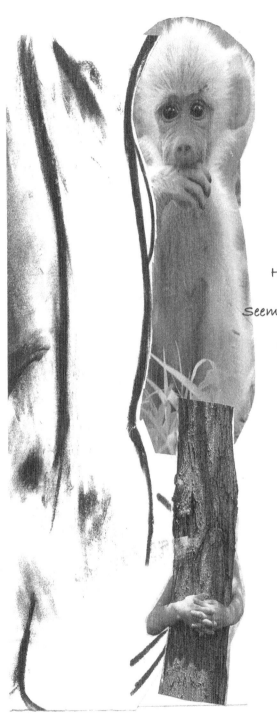

Unspoken Void

Groundless

Holding on for life

Seems the right thing to do

But I forget why

CHAPTER ONE

A DEVELOPMENTAL PERSPECTIVE

So why, after my partner and I had weathered other disruptions and difficulties over the years, was the insertion of a person in our working environment so debilitating? Because the "secure" attachment I had formed was threatened, and I was left with no solid ground to stand upon. .

What happens to children who do not form secure attachments? Research suggests that failure to form secure attachments early in life can have a negative impact on behavior in later childhood and throughout life.

The developmental approach to recovery views Codependency as a failure to complete certain crucial developmental tasks – particularly bonding and separation – during the first 6 years of life. This results in issues which extend across the life span.

As a result of incomplete bonding and/or separateness a person will get stuck:

1. Trying to compete bonding by expending a great deal of anxious energy monitoring potential threats to the attachment (Anxious/Ambivalent Codependency)

    Or

2. Trying to complete separation and autonomy by being very unattached or avoiding intimacy to prevent the pain of broken attachment (Avoidant/Dismissive Codependency)

    Or

3. Cycling back and forth between these two Codependency styles, both developed in response to disrupted early attachments..

In this developmental model, painful and anxiety producing life events are seen as developmental crises rather than emotional breakdowns or mental illness. This perspective allows us to form a more optimistic picture of healing for people suffering from Codependency by addressing all three key areas (developmental, behavioral, and biological).

What's Your Attachment Style? Here's a Quiz

I have included this questionnaire to help prepare for the following discussion on the developmental origins of codependency. Today's attachment researchers find it helpful to look at the proportion of anxiety and avoidance that we experience in relation to emotional intimacy. Allow yourself about twenty minutes in total and grab a calculator because the scoring is a bit tricky. Don't worry, you'll get the idea. If you are currently in emotional pain, you may just want to review the questions to "get the gist" of where I am going in this section. Enjoy your internal exploration.

The Experiences in Close Relationships-Revised (ECR-R) Questionnaire; Fraley, Waller, and Brennan (2000)

The statements below concern how you feel in emotionally intimate relationships. Answer the questions in terms of how you *generally* experience relationships, not just in what is happening in a current relationship. Respond to each statement by giving a number from 1 through 7 to indicate how much you agree or disagree with the statement. 1 = strongly disagree and 7 = strongly agree. At the end of the survey, you will find scoring instructions. Trust me. You can get through this. Use a calculator. Or, again, you can bag scoring the test at all!

1. strongly disagree
2. disagree
3. disagree somewhat
4. neutral

5. agree somewhat

6. agree

7. strongly agree

1. It's not difficult for me to get close to my partner.
   4   4
2. I often worry that my partner will not want to stay with me.
   7
3. I often worry that my partner doesn't really love me.
   5
4. It helps to turn to my romantic partner in times of need.
   5   3
5. I often wish that my partner's feelings for me were as strong as my feelings for him or her.
   2
6. I worry a lot about my relationships.
   6
7. I feel comfortable depending on romantic partners.
   6   2
8. When I show my feelings for romantic partners, I'm afraid they will not feel the same about me.
   7
9. I rarely worry about my partner leaving me.
   1   7
10. My partner only seems to notice me when I'm angry.
    2
11. I feel comfortable depending on romantic partners.
    6   2
12. I do not often worry about being abandoned.
    6   2
13. My romantic partner makes me doubt myself.
    5
14. I find that my partner(s) don't want to get as close as I would like.
    1
15. I'm afraid that I will lose my partner's love.
    5
16. My desire to be very close sometimes scares people away.
    1
17. I worry that I won't measure up to other people.
    5
18. I find it easy to depend on romantic partners.
    4   4

19. I prefer not to show a partner how I feel deep down.
7

20. I feel comfortable sharing my private thoughts and feelings with my partner.
5   3

21. I worry that romantic partners won't care about me as much as I care about them.
4

22. I find it difficult to allow myself to depend on romantic partners.
5

23. I'm afraid that once a romantic partner gets to know me, he or she won't like who I really am.
6

24. I am very comfortable being close to romantic partners.
3   5

25. I don't feel comfortable opening up to romantic partners.
5

26. I prefer not to be too close to romantic partners.
4

27. I get uncomfortable when a romantic partner wants to be very close.
6

28. I find it relatively easy to get close to my partner.
3   5

29. I usually discuss my problems and concerns with my partner.
5   3

30. I tell my partner just about everything.
4   4

31. Sometimes romantic partners change their feelings about me for no apparent reason.
3

32. When my partner is out of sight, I worry that he or she might become interested in someone else.
6

33. I am nervous when partners get too close to me.
5

34. It's easy for me to be affectionate with my partner.
2   6

35. It makes me mad that I don't get the affection and support I need from my partner.
4

36. My partner really understands me and my needs.
5   3

Scoring:

1. Some answers need to be reverse scored like this: 1=7, 2=6, 3=5, 4=4, 5=3, 6=2, 7=1. Take all the numerical answers to the following questions and give them a new, reversed score: 1, 4, 7, 9, 11, 12, 18, 20, 24, 28, 29, 30, 34, 36.

2. Take the scores to all the following question numbers and average them. These are the questions you should average: 2, 3, 5, 6, 8, 9, 10, 12, 13, 14, 15, 16, 17, 21, 23, 31, 32, 35. In case you're rusty on third grade math, that means add them all together and divide by the number of answers, in this case, 18. This is your score for attachment-related anxiety. It can range from 1 through 7. The higher the number, the more anxious you are about relationships.

3. ④ Take the scores to the following questions and average them: 1, 4, 7, 11, 18, 19, 20, 22, 24, 25, 26, 27, 28, 29, 30, 33, 34, 36). This score indicates you attachment related avoidance. The higher the score, the more you avoid intimacy in relationships.

③.8 Again, many of us score in both ranges, swinging from one level of connection to the other over time. The key is that in both cases, we do not trust that the attachment is secure.

The Developmental section that follows outlines the contribution of research to our understanding of the developmental process of attachment. I'll discuss its significance and how it translates from childhood models to adult relationships. I rewrote this section to clarify important points as we go along. I know that if you are in the kind of pain I was in when writing it, your mind may wander at times, so you may have to go back to review occasionally. That's fine. Be kind to yourself and remember it will be worth your while.

The behavioral section outlines the behaviors and areas to consider in healing. The biological portion looks at the toll the stress of attachment disruption can take on our bodies. Trust me, this is important to read. Even if you have to put it down now and again because it seems "too much." I felt the same way writing it, but I had much greater self-compassion when I finished. Hopefully, you will too.

We will start with Attachment Theory

Why Does Attachment Matter?

Secure bonding and attachment between caregivers and their children sets the foundation for our future connections with others. **Bonding** generally refers to the parents' emotional investment in their child, which builds and grows with repeated meaningful shared experiences. **Attachment** usually refers to the tie between the infant and parents, which the child actively initiates and participates in. The quality of attachment largely determines the child's developing sense of self and approach to the world environment.

Psychologist John Bowlby, the first attachment theorist, describes attachment as a "lasting psychological connectedness between human beings." (1)

Beginning with John Bowlby (2), Attachment Theory offers the following themes:

1. A psychology based on the opposing tendencies of attachment and separation/loss. There is always a tension between our need to feel connected and have roots, and our need to develop which will push us out of our "safe" zone. I would argue that we need one (safety) to fully embrace the other (separation).

2. The individual's need for secure attachment in order to successfully reach out and explore one's inner world and outer environment. Knowing I have a safe harbor allows me to risk entering deeper waters, trusting that when I come home to familiar waters I will recognize myself and the people who love me who are waiting for me to return.

3. The persistence of attachment needs throughout life. Bowlby points out that we never outgrow the need for secure attachments. Having a "home base" is key to personal and professional development, whereas lack of a home base can create almost intolerable anxiety.

4.   The negative consequences of early disruption of bonding or attachment. Research shows early disruption of our ability to trust our attachments to others has life-long consequences. Up to 2/3 of people maintain consistent attachment style from childhood to adult relationships.

5.   The caregiver's capacity to maintain loving presence and to accept protest is of vital importance to a child's mental health. *Accept protest* means letting the child express anger and frustration openly and without loss of parental love or intimacy.

Researchers point out that the ability to withstand separation has not had the same focus as establishing the original attachment. Yet, clinicians like Mary Ainsworth point out the parent's ability to accept protest without retaliation or excessive anxiety is a key determinant of secure attachment. (3) The child must be welcomed back with *unconditional* intimacy. Parent's must resolve their own attachment needs in order to tolerate the child's growing need to differentiate (establish a "self" apart from the parent). Anxiously attached parents are threatened by the child's needs for "space" and may smother them, whereas avoidantly attached parents find the child's resistance or protests painful and then withdraw from the child.

What does it look like when a parent cannot connect this way due to her own interrupted attachment history?

Little Jeremy is quietly playing with his blocks, occasionally looking over to the kitchen to make sure his mom is still there. Mom is preoccupied while doing last night's dishes. She is tired of her husband's drinking and feels like saying something, but she dreads the fight that will unfold when she does. She looks over and sees Jeremy playing and has an urge to hug him, unaware that she is looking for comfort for herself. As she reaches out to pick Jeremy up he protests, wanting to continue playing with his toys.

Mom reacts as though she has been slapped by Jeremy. Feeling rejected, she roughly drops him back to the floor and heads back to the bedroom. Jeremy notices she is leaving and becomes anxious. He starts to cry for her. Angry with Jeremy, mom lets him cry for a while to "punish" him before returning to the den to pick him up.

We need to bond without being swallowed up. This contributes to our development of autonomy and creativity.

We need to separate without feeling abandoned. Caregivers remain attentive to the child's cues for reengagement.

Secure attachments develop as a result of consistent and accurate response between the caregiver and child. This requires the caregiver to be emotionally, cognitively, and physically present in a predictable and meaningful way in order to participate in the developing relationship over time.

Characteristics of Attachment

- **Safe Haven:** When the child feel threatened or afraid, he or she can return to the caregiver for comfort and soothing.

- **Secure Base:** The caregiver provides a secure and dependable base for the child to explore the world.

- **Proximity Maintenance:** The child strives to stay near the caregiver, thus keeping the child safe.

- **Separation Distress:** When separated from the caregiver, the child will become upset and distressed.

Parental attunement and responsiveness has been documented on a physiological level as well. The heart rates of securely attached infants and their mothers in the Ainsworth's "Strange Situation" (See Appendix) parallel each other, whereas they do not with insecurely attached infants and their mothers (4). The mirroring of heart rates indicates the mother's sensitivity and involvement in her infant's perceived experience. Mothers of secure infants pick their babies up more quickly when they see signs of distress, play with them more, and generally seem more aware of them and their needs than parents of insecure infants. One such need is to be able to play "alone in the presence of the mother." To meet this need the mother must be capable of providing an unobtrusive background which enables self-exploration. (5) If the child is repeatedly interrupted by a demanding caregiver who seeks comfort and validation from the child, the child becomes prematurely and compulsively attuned to the demands of others. This child loses awareness of its own spontaneous needs and develops a false sense of self based on compliance and competence in meeting the needs of his/her caregivers.

Michele is the youngest of five children. Her mother had been over stressed with no extended family support and the family lived in survival mode throughout Michele's childhood. Due to financial hardship and time limitations, Michele was not able to participate in after school activities and never had the chance to pursue her desire to take dancing lessons. Once Michele became a parent she swore that her children would never miss out on an opportunity. It creates enormous conflict between Michele and her daughter, Amber, when her daughter begs to stay home and play with her toy ponies instead of go to Gymboree class. Amber is realizing that her mommy becomes very sad and withdrawn for the rest of the night if Amber doesn't go to class, and then she feels sad herself. Amber misses her mom and begins to go to class without complaining so her mommy will be "happy" and then play with her the rest of the night.

Pediatrician and Psychoanalyst D.W. Winnicott pointed out that the need for privacy and occasional freedom from structure for "unstructured play" are necessary over the course of the life span. In childhood this is crucial to develop a *self*. (6) We never outgrow the need to regroup and think our own thoughts, just as we never outgrow the need for attachment and a secure base from which to explore the world.

Secure attachment is associated with an internalized sense of lovability, of being worthy of care, of being effective in eliciting care when required, and a sense of personal efficacy in dealing with most stressors independently. Secure preschoolers develop an understanding of other people's thoughts and emotions, leading to empathy (7).

The implications of this are powerful!

When I can TRUST the people close to me, I translate this to mean I am WORTH being loved and cared about. Because I have the "safety net" created by a trusted support system I feel like I can tackle stressors in my life and be effective. Because my caregivers

have been accurately attuned to me emotionally and reflected my thoughts back to me accurately, I can TRUST myself to read the thoughts and feelings of others accurately because I recognize those thoughts and feelings. The ability to recognize and share in the feelings of others is empathy.

When we don't have this secure foundation we become anxiously attached codependents who don't trust the attachment of and fear that they will abandon us, or we become avoidantly attached codependents who don't allow ourselves to attach to or depend on those who will "inevitably" leave us. Ultimately we are not attuned to ourselves or others and we translate that to mean we aren't worth being loved or attended to. This leads to life-long patterns of self-abandonment.

When Attachment Gets Interrupted

There are so many reasons that early attachment can get interrupted. Below are a few of the more common reasons:

- Extended periods of illness (parent or child)
- Hospitalization due to physical or mental illness
- Placement in the foster care system
- Serious mental illness creating emotional and mental unavailability
- Abusive relationships that absorb the majority of the caretaker's energy
- Incarceration
- Alcohol/Drug addiction
- Military service

None of these reasons have anything to do with LOVE for the child. Unfortunately the child cannot possibly know this. The child winds up believing that the unavailable parent is not available due to some defect within the child. We believe that if we were "enough" the parent would CHOOSE to be available.

This begins the "going to the hardware store to get milk" pattern we talk about in Al-Anon. In this analogy, we go to the hardware store to get milk, which is not sold at hardware stores. When we realize milk is not available we:

- protest and demand more loudly that they get milk for us assuming they aren't listening or taking our needs seriously
- accuse them of having milk but withholding it from us
- believe that they would give us milk if we were somehow different or better

Sanity returns when we acknowledge that the store is not withholding milk but simply does not have it to sell. In reality, many of us spend years of our lives using every tool possible to "force" a response from our parents that they are not capable of giving. When we learn that they do not have it to give, we can stop futile demands that increasingly damage the relationship and our self-esteem over time. We can learn to accept what people CAN give rather than focus on what they are not capable of giving.

Amy has fought all her life for her mother's approval. She overhears her mother tell other people how proud she is of Amy, yet the direct feedback she receives consists of warnings to "not get too big for her britches," or not to "count her chickens before their hatched" whenever Amy announces a new professional undertaking. When Amy was honored as valedictorian in high school, her mother pointed out that there would be smarter kids at the college when Amy got there. She reminded Amy, "Don't think that just because you are a big fish in a little pond that there aren't bigger fish." Amy pushed herself so hard at work that she began to have conflicts with her coworkers, and her boss gently recommended that Amy see an Employee Assistance Counselor. By the second visit, the Counselor was clear that Amy would need longer term support and recommended a therapist that specialized in codependency issues.

Through the course of therapy, Amy began to explore her mother's history as a child which had been filled with lost dreams and broken promises. Her mother had closed off her heart to "possibility" a long time ago, and it became clear to Amy that her mother saw herself as protective of Amy by offering her such discouraging feedback. Over time, she learned that her mother was not capable of celebrating success with Amy, terrified that something would happen and Amy would get her heart broken the way she had earlier in life. Amy would need to seek out people who were not so afraid to share her latest business ideas. It was not that her mother didn't love her or wasn't proud, she was simply too wounded and too scared to risk feeling Amy's joy.

Characteristics of Anxious or Ambivalent Attachment

(Anxious Codependent)

Research suggests that anxious attachment is a result of poor maternal availability or inconsistent responsiveness to the child. These children cannot depend on their mother (or caregiver) to respond in a consistent or timely manner when the child is in need or experiencing distress.

These parents tend to be poorly attuned to their children's needs, often ignoring them when they are distressed and intruding on them when they are playing contentedly. These parents offer interrupted or inconsistent parental care. When the parent feels calm, she responds to her child in a sensitive way; when she is angry, she expresses it openly with yelling and perhaps hitting. The parent's responses are internally consistent for them, but unfortunately unpredictable to anyone else, especially the child. ***The child feels powerless to control or predict his/her experience*** because the response will be unpredictably either supportive or hostile which may create learned helplessness and limit risk taking and exploration.

This is an impossible situation to maneuver because the rules for conduct and parental expectations are always shifting based on the caregiver's emotional regulation skills. I can go to hug my mom after school today and she will be either neutral or positive. However, when I do the same thing tomorrow I might be met with a hostile response: "Why are you bothering me? Leave me alone!"

Martin has always wanted children, promising himself that he would provide a different childhood than he had experienced with his alcoholic father.

When his own son, Jorge, was born it was the happiest day of Martin's life. Martin never drinks to make sure his new son has it "better than I had." Unfortunately, without alcohol (Martin's only stress-management tool) Martin is increasingly moody and unpredictable at home. His wife, Lucia, spends a lot of energy trying to anticipate Martin's mood, including calling him before he leaves work to "get the lay of the land." Jorge, who is now 3 years old, adores his father and lights up the room every time he sees him. Some of the time, Martin is equally thrilled to see his son, no matter what kind of day he has had. However, sometimes when Jorge runs up to the door, Martin is sharp with him – roughly dismisses him by telling him to "go away and play," or yells for Lucia to "come get the boy" in obvious annoyance at the child's demands. Jorge is crushed when this happens, and is confused. While Lucia tries to comfort him, Jorge still feels like he did something wrong by bothering his daddy.

Even when the child can force closeness and attention from the caregiver, once obtained it is often not soothing and may be punishing. Consequently the child remains persistently anxious or angry.

Because of the intermittent reinforcement for turning to the attachment figure for security (sometimes they respond and sometimes they don't), the need to be vigilant for her presence and loss is strongly reinforced. **The child's confidence in itself to respond appropriately to threats and self-soothe does not develop adequately** as all of its coping mechanisms are being developed to manage external threats to security. This sets the foundation for later external choices to manage our anxiety, such as alcohol, drugs, or pornography. Certainly we are learning that trusting the people close to us will not be a realistic option, and more than likely we will pick relationships in the future that will reinforce that trust is not possible by picking unavailable, unpredictable partners.

Case Example:

An extreme example of this rage and impulsiveness was demonstrated by Clara Harris, who became overwhelmed by the threat of abandonment by her husband, David.

Clara Harris is an accomplished dentist and business woman, who was seen by others to be extremely competent, family-oriented, and even controlling. In 2002, Clara Harris discovered her husband, co-owner of their six successful dental practices, was carrying on an affair with the receptionist, Gail Bridges, a divorcee with three children of her own. As soon as Clara Harris found out about her husband's affair she did everything she could think of to save her marriage, which included willingness to lose herself and merge into her projection of her husband's fantasy partner. She:

- obtained detailed information from her husband on what attracted him to the other woman
- had a heart-to-heart talk with her husband about their marital problems.
- went to a salon and had her hair cut and lightened to blonde
- had her nails done
- joined a gym / health club
- hired a personal trainer.
- made a $5000 deposit for breast augmentation surgery and liposuction
- cooked her husband's favorite meals
- began having sex with him at least 3 times each night
- went shopping for sexy clothes
- bought seductive lingerie from Victoria's Secret
- took a leave of absence from her job at the couple's chain of dental clinics so she could devote all her time to her husband
- fired her husband's mistress, who worked as a receptionist at the same dental clinic as her husband
- persuaded her husband to agree to end his affair with the other woman
- had her stepdaughter buy her 2 relationship books
- hired a private investigator
- discussed seeing a marriage counselor

A truly anxious/ambivalent Codependent, Clara Harris did all this in the space of 7 days, wasting no time. She found out about the affair on July 16th, and her husband confessed to the affair on July 17th. Clara's efforts to save her marriage might have succeeded, but by July 24th, David Harris was dead. Intent on doing everything she could to save her marriage from the day she discovered his infidelity until the day David Harris was killed, Clara was unable to tolerate evidence that the affair had continued and the attachment remained threatened.

Clara Harris confronted her husband with his lover at a hotel. She then went outside, got in her Mercedes and proceeded to run over her husband again and again, circling the car over different parts of his body, crushing his legs, ribs and head. An eye witness to the crime stated that when Clara finished, she got out of her car and, in a final burst of anger, leaned over her husband's mangled, crushed body as he exhaled his last breath. "See what you made me do!" she screamed.

When interviewed later, it was clear that Clara had loved her husband "more than life" and just wanted to stop the pain she was feeling. Obliterating him was an attempt to obliterate her pain.

Characteristics of Avoidant or Dismissive Attachment

(Avoidant Codependent)

Research indicates that when caregivers are consistently non-responsive, or even punishing when children seek closeness these children will show no preference between a caregiver and a complete stranger. *Children who are punished for relying on a caregiver will learn to avoid seeking help in the future.*

These parents are more brusque and functional in their handling, unresponsive to their child's needs or intolerant of a child's distress. Grossmann and Grossmann (8) studied parental interaction with babies identified as avoidant at 12 and 18 months. *Parents of avoidant babies interfered when their babies were already engrossed in play,*

and withdrew when their babies expressed negative feelings, especially toward the caregiver. The children showed many expressions of uncertainty toward continued play. By contrast, parents of securely attached infants engaged in mutual play when the baby appeared to be at a loss for what to do next but watched quietly (with interest) when the infants did not need them. The avoidant child learns that seeking closeness through crying and clinging is futile. It actually results in parental withdrawal. Independence is reinforced and valued instead. As a result, attachment behaviors are relatively diminished and detachment behaviors become prominent.

Cherise was stunned when her husband announced his intention to file for divorce and move in with her best friend. Cherise was almost immobilized with grief now that she had lost BOTH people in her life she trusted. Managing two children, 5 and 7 years old, was overwhelming. Sammy, her 7 year old, looked very much like his father and had many of his mannerisms. There were times when his tone of voice or facial expression was a carbon copy of his father. Sammy was tearful and uncooperative with Cherise when she could muster up the energy to interact with him, which discouraged her from even trying. It was clear to both children that when they needed something it made mommy angry and she was "mean," especially to Sammy. Sammy learned to make breakfast for he and his sister instead of asking for help. He learned to help his sister get dressed before school, and encouraged her to "play quietly" when they were home so mommy could rest.

Maintaining physical closeness to the caregiver is necessary for any child's protection and nurturing, and a child's natural tendency is to withdraw from a perceived threat and approach the caretaker for safety and comforting. However, the avoidant child's caretaker (i.e., mother) *is* the threat, and punishes the approaching child with rejection. Thus, the child has learned to avoid any communication of dependence, presenting an irresolvable conflict between their instincts for safety and comfort and the pain of rejection. This lays the foundation for the increased detachment from their internal world which is so present in avoidant adults.

The Avoidant Codependent conflict is this: I *want* to allow myself to depend on someone who SAYS they love me, but my *experience* is whenever I become vulnerable or "needy" I get abandoned and hurt. So, I allow myself to attach to others to a point but always have a "Plan B" prepared for the inevitable disappointment of rejection. Of course the very act of having a "Plan B" means that I never fully ante up – I am never all the way "in" which leads to the separation. I'm convinced is inevitable anyway. I may be manifesting the very thing I fear most.

Marlene has been in a long distance relationship with Raj for the last two years and for most of that time has driven three hours to see him every weekend. To make this more comfortable, she has stored clothing and some personal effects at his home to make travel easier. Raj is very much in love with Marlene and has expressed often that he would like to have her move in with him and "take this relationship to the next level," including marriage. This creates tremendous anxiety for Marlene as she pictures herself being "swallowed up" by Raj, completely dependent on him in a new environment. As she agrees to this plan, she arranges to store all of her furniture rather than sell it on Craig's list, "just in case" everything goes south and she has to start all over again. In the process of making arrangements to move, Raj and Marlene start fighting every weekend. This triggers Marlene to finally say, "Forget it. I KNEW if I let myself depend on you, you would become a control freak" and break up with him.

In reality the act of detaching emotionally from relationships as protection is an empty gesture. Research (9) with surviving family members of victims of suicide or accidental death indicate that the most grief-stricken survivors were more detached from family than those who were least grief stricken. The detached survivors actually had more unresolved in their relationships, which created greater grief when the opportunity for resolution was suddenly and permanently denied. Remorse compounds the loss.

Avoidant Codependents are not obvious in that they may have a variety of social connections. They may have been children who used compensating strategies of compulsive caregiving, in which the child reassures the withdrawn and depressed parent that everything is all right, or compulsive compliance, in which the child becomes highly vigilant to the hostile and unpredictable parent's desires and complies promptly with them. These children may become "parenti-fied" as a caretaker for their parent and may be able to anticipate and comply with the parent's needs before they are even formulated. (10, 11) Ultimately they become adolescents and adults who are emotion-ally insulated, intimacy-phobic and "compulsively self-reliant." (12) A consequence of this insulation is isolation. The underlying incen-tive for the avoiding aspect of detachment is fear of intimacy.

Carolyn has been staying home from school when her mother has a migraine since she was in elementary school. Her mother's migraines began shortly after her divorce and Carolyn's mother would become immobilized by her migraine, unable to take care of household responsibilities. Carolyn learned to anticipate the "signs" of an impending headache usually triggered by stress. She became very adept at managing her own meals and homework, asking for very little input from her mother. In fact, when her mother would come home from work, Carolyn would usually have dinner prepared and would spend whatever time was necessary listening as mom processed her day. Carolyn discovered she missed far less time at school when she adhered to this routine, so would turn down invitations to other people's homes if it would make her unavailable for her mother. Carolyn's mother consistently told others how close she felt to Carolyn as they "shared everything" with each other. In reality, Carolyn's mother knew very little about her daughter as they both ignored Carolyn's internal world.

CHAPTER TWO

CODEPENDENCY AND ATTACHMENT THEORY

I am certainly not the first to make the connection between codependency and attachment theory. Zimberoff and Hartman (13) indicate in their research that

> *"the child who is repeatedly interrupted by a demanding caregiver, i.e., through the parental impingement phenomenon, becomes compulsively attuned to the demands of others, losing awareness of its own spontaneous needs and developing a false sense of self based on compliance and performance. This infant experiences his/her parents (and thus the world) as dangerous and frightening. This can be the genesis of codependency in adulthood... Seriously insecure attachment creates a dissociated core of the self, an absence of self. It reflects a breach in the boundaries of the self..."*

Author Dr. Tian Dayton (14) provides her own definition of codependency using an integration of attachment theory (and Bowen family systems theory):

> *Codependency, I feel, is fear-based and is a predictable set of qualities and behaviors that grow out of feeling anxious and therefore hypervigilant in our intimate relationships. It is also reflective of an incomplete process of individuation....Though codependency seems to be about caretaking or being overly attuned to the other person, it is really about trying to fend off our own anxiety"*

Dr. Dayton believes that codependency and counterdependency (what I am labeling avoidant/dismissive attachment) are the result of attachment injuries, or relationship traumas as she calls it.

In his seminal book, *The Road Less Traveled,* M. Scott Peck explores the roles of fear of abandonment. Self-care – or the ability to recognize that you will get what you want only if you do some of the job your-self – is learned in the face of the child's elemental desire to be cared for totally. Our fundamental desire to merge struggles with the need to develop competence. Competence is scary, because it may indicate to our caretakers that we are ready to be "on our own" and we may find ourselves prematurely self-sufficient. Developing initiative and skills does not have to result in abandonment. With a secure home base we can venture out and return, trusting there will be a consistent welcome.

> *Most parents, even when they are otherwise relatively ignorant or callous, are instinctively sensitive to their children's fear of abandonment and will therefore, day in and day out, hundreds and thousands of times, offer their children needed reassurance: "You know Mommy and Daddy aren't going to leave you behind"; "Of course Mommy and Daddy will come back to get you"; "Mommy and Daddy aren't going to forget about you!" If these words are matched by deeds, month in and month out, year in and year out, by the time of adolescence, the child will have lost the fear of abandonment and in its stead will have a deep inner feeling that the world is a safe place in which to be, and protection will be there when it is needed. With this internal sense of the consistent safety of the world, such a child is free to delay gratification of one kind or another, secure in the knowledge that the opportunity for gratification, like home and parents, is always there, available when needed....(15)*

Internal Working Models

The construct to explain how the early attachment experiences become long-term, lifelong traits is that of **internal working models**. With repetition over time, the infant is conditioned into generalizing his/her experiences into expectations for future relationship experience. Internal working models serve to regulate, interpret, and predict the parent/child attachment-related behavior, thoughts, and feelings in situations of loss, threat, isolation and dependency. A child constructs a working model of itself as valued and competent when parents as emotionally available and supportive of exploratory activities.

Samuel loves children and was thrilled to have both a son and a daughter. As his daughter, Sarah, becomes 9 years old she begins to struggle in math. Samuel has always loved math and at first he is confused by her apparent inability to master what, to him, are simple concepts. However, Samuel knows Sarah is bright and commits to patiently working with her every evening. In the process Samuel is communicating to Sarah that she is capable, that she CAN do the math, and he is committed to supporting her efforts even if it means hiring a tutor. Sarah is very clear that her struggle in math is completely separate from her value as a person and her father's attention and support are not conditional. Sarah's working model will be "I ask for support and I am responded to without shame." This will bode very well for her when she begins to look for a boyfriend because boys who speak to her with respect will be natural choices for her.

Conversely, a working model of self as devalued and incompetent develops from parents who are rejecting or ignoring thus interfering with exploration. The models of self and parents develop together, as complements of each other, and represent both sides of the relationship. (16)

Healthy development requires a child to update internal working models over time. In fact, "Bowlby repeatedly warned of the pathogenic [illness causing] potential of working models that are not updated" (17). The expectations of one's parents and oneself at age one certainly adjusts and expands by age three, or ten, or eighteen. A parent may "reform," becoming more able to respond to his/her child's needs when life circumstances improve, leading the child to construct revised working models of self as valued and of parents as caring.

Manuel has spent the first 6 years of his son's life in and out of addiction rehabilitation centers. Manuel loves his son, Juan, very much but has broken many promises and has not been reliable. He knows Juan loves him also, but Juan is a little afraid of him and worries about whether or not Manuel will do what he promises to do. Manuel is committed to sobriety at this point in his life and has maintained 2 years clean and sober. The longer he remains sober the more he notices that Juan doesn't call him so many times to "remind" him before he visits. He notices that the transition between visits is smoother as Juan no longer clings to him, afraid he won't see Manuel again. The stronger the relationship with Juan becomes the more deeply committed Manuel is to his sobriety, realizing that he can have the relationship with Juan that he never had with his own father.

However, there is built-in resistance to changing models once they have become habitual and automatic. Expectations become self-fulfilling through biased expectations of upcoming experiences with parents, and through the process of relationship consistency (18). A parent's occasional failure to attend is not likely to undermine a child's confidence in their emotional availability, nor is her parent's occasional healthy caregiving likely to overcome a child's learned insecurity.

Eventually, the internal working models that drive our ways of acting and thinking become unconscious (inaccessible to consciousness) and thus inflexible and reactive.

The family experience of those who grow up anxious and fearful is characterized not only by uncertainty about parental support, but also by subtle yet strongly distorting parental pressures. For example, pressure on the child to act as caregiver for a parent; or to adopt, and thereby to confirm, a parent's working models of self, of child and of their relationship.

Jackie has known from a very young age that her parents worry a great deal about how they are seen as demonstrated by the familiar mantra, "What will people think?" Jackie is acutely aware of her mother's dependency on her pills, what she calls her "nerve medicine," and her mother frequently forgets obligations or even full sentences in the evening. Jackie is especially afraid to drive in the evening with her mother because her mother tends to drift into other lanes as she chats away oblivious to the havoc she is creating around her. Rather than address the pill abuse that creates this dangerous situation, Jackie points out that her mother's eyesight seems to be less sharp at night. She repeats this so often it becomes a family belief, and her father begins to do the driving in the evening. Jackie is well aware that an open discussion of a family "problem" would be met with denial and most likely she would be identified as having a bad attitude.

The family experience of those who grow up to become relatively secure and self-reliant is characterized not only by unfailing parental support but also by a steady yet timely encouragement toward increasing autonomy. There is a frank communication by parents of their working models, their expectations for relationship rules and structure for themselves, for the child and for others. These working models are not only acknowledged but are open to be questioned and revised.

Brett and his sister Joyce have always enjoyed visits to their grandparent's house in the summer. They are able to fish and swim in the lake. Their grandparents are obviously thrilled to spend the time with them. Brett and Joyce have become increasingly worried about their single dad, Mike. He seems quiet, preoccupied, and can't remember his commitments. Last week he forgot to pick up Brett after baseball and another parent took him home. They share their concerns with their grandparents, Mike's parents, and the grandparents become concerned. They are hearing signs of depression that they knew Mike had struggled with when the children were younger. When their dad comes for a visit, the family sits down to have dinner and the grandparent's help the children to tell their dad what they are noticing and tell him they are worried. Mike is able to hear their concerns without becoming angry and, after his initial denial, agrees to see a doctor.

One defense Sometimes when our experience does not match the acceptable "reality" our parents pressure us to adopt, one defense is to change the model by changing the identity of the person (e.g., an attachment figure) involved. For example, a child may divert hostile feelings toward the parent which are inconsistent with the parent's working model of relationships, toward another less formidable person like a neighbor or a coach. *Obviously Daddy can't be unavailable – the coach is stupid for scheduling the game at that time.*

Some children produce defensive self-blame by taking anger they initially felt toward the attachment figure and redirect it towards themselves. *Daddy would be available if I was smarter.*

They may compulsively attempt to offer caregiving to others (including the parent), diverting attention from their own unmet attachment needs. *If I make Daddy laugh or bring him his beer he might want to come to my games.*

The child's response to negative parental treatment can be generalized as follows: **The avoidant/dismissive child develops a deactivating strategy to ward off stressful experiences. The anxious/ambivalent child develops a hypervigilance strategy to detect and disarm them.**

These patterns, while deeply embedded in the unconscious, remain active in driving behavioral choices. This is the general foundation for adult codependency.

Internal working models can be changed over time, as documented by changes in attachment classification. However, changing working models requires the individual to reassess some deeply embedded beliefs. The more deeply embedded the working model, the more profound any change becomes. Changing a working model based on early traumatic events requires revisions and reinterpretations of many related assumptions and beliefs.

That in turn requires enough security to risk the freedom to explore one's fundamental foundations. Thus, changing one's working model requires us to uncover our early experiences and create "corrective experiences" to replace the originally embedded fearful ones. (19) For example, hypervigilance based on parental inconsistency in childhood (e.g., "I expect my mother to explode in rage unpredictably any moment"), would need to be corrected by current experiences of secure attachments in the present that are predictable. My defense mechanism, hypervigilance, would no longer be necessary if my relationship choices became healthier.

Debbie has been seeing a therapist to treat her Post Traumatic Stress symptoms developed in response to a 10-year relationship. During those 10 years her children had experienced her as irritable, having mood swings, over reacting when startled and yelling, having physical pain which made her too tired to play with them and occasional periods where she would not get off the couch. However, as Debbie participates in her support groups, sees a

therapist and is stabilized on medication she is becoming far more predict-
able. When the children have to give her "bad news" like a poor school grade,
she is able to get into solution with the child and work to improve the grade.
When she is having a difficult day, she is able to tell the children what is
happening rather than acting it out in rejecting ways so they will leave her
alone. Over time, the children notice that they are more comfortable having
friends over to the house, and don't worry about her when they are gone.
In fact, they are starting to take her for granted the way most children take
their parent's for granted. In Debbie's case, it is a good sign when they
forget to call on time because they are paying attention to their own lives
instead of monitoring her!

CHAPTER THREE

ATTACHMENT PATTERNS OVER THE LIFESPAN

Attachment and Psychological Openness

One of the signs of resilience in life is flexibility, and not surprisingly secure attachment is correlated with cognitive openness – the ability to tolerate ambiguity and the freedom to integrate new information and perspectives. Anxious people are often preoccupied by the threatening aspects of new information. Avoidant people overemphasize self-reliance, and so habitually reject any new information that might demand a revision of their beliefs. If you think about yourself or people you know, you'll see this makes sense intuitively.

One of the reasons we find people who have "reformed" (e.g. stopped smoking) so irritating is their cognitive rigidity. Because they haven't fully accepted themselves as a "non-smoker" they are highly agitated by, or even hostile to, those who still smoke. They can be outrageously rude and judgmental, making exaggerated coughing sounds, or waving their hands in front of their face in an offensive manner when encountering a smoker. This is also true of newly recovering alcoholics, who INSIST that the only true path to recovery is the path they are following. They can become intrusive "Big Book" thumpers who frequently quote the Big Book of Alcoholics Anonymous to chide a fellow recovering person who appears to the newly recovering alcoholic to be "off track."

When we are truly secure in our view of self, we lose our need to "force" others to adopt a similar view in order to validate or approve of us. We can easily tolerate our differences and express curiosity rather than act threatened, or pretend we don't notice them.

Adult Working Models of Attachment

Bartholomew and Horowitz have proposed that working models consist of two parts (20). One part deals with thoughts about the self. The other part deals with thoughts about others. They further propose that a person's thoughts about self are generally positive or generally negative. The same applies to a person's thoughts about others. Thoughts about others are generally positive or generally negative.

Baldwin and colleagues have applied the theory of relational schemas to working models of attachment. Relational schemas contain information about the way partners regularly interact with each other. (21, 22)

For each pattern of interaction that regularly occurs between partners, a relational schema is formed that contains:

- Information about the self.
- Information about the partner.
- Information about the way the interaction usually unfolds.

For example, if a person regularly asks his or her partner for a hug or kiss, and the partner regularly responds with a hug or kiss, the person forms a relational schema representing this predictable interaction. The schema contains information about the self (e.g., "I need lots of physical affection"). It also contains information about the partner (e.g., "My partner is an affectionate person"). And it contains information about the way the interaction usually unfolds, which can be summarized by an IF-THEN statement (e.g., "IF I ask my partner for a hug or kiss, THEN my partner will respond with a hug or kiss and comfort me"). Relational schemas help guide behavior in relationships by allowing people to anticipate and plan for partner responses.

This information about the way interactions usually unfold is the unique contribution of relational schemas to working models. Relational schemas add the IF-THEN statements about interactions to working models. To demonstrate how working models are organized as relational schemas, Baldwin and colleagues created a set of written scenarios that described interactions dealing with trust, dependency and closeness.(23)

For example, the scenarios for closeness included:

- You want to spend more time with your partner.
- You reach out to hug or kiss your partner.
- You tell your partner how deeply you feel for him or her.

Following each scenario, people were presented with two options about how their partners might respond. One option was "he/she accepts you." The other option was "he/she rejects you." People were asked to rate the likelihood of each response on a seven point scale. Ratings of likely partner responses corresponded to people's attachment styles. People with secure attachment styles were more likely to expect accepting responses from their partners. Their relational schema for the third closeness scenario would be, "IF I tell my partner how deeply I feel for him or her, THEN my partner will accept me." People with other attachment styles were less likely to expect accepting responses from their partners. Their relational schema for the third closeness scenario would be, "IF I tell my partner how deeply I feel for him or her, THEN my partner will reject me." Differences in attachment styles reflect differences in relational schemas. Relational schemas may therefore be used to understand the organization of working models of attachment as has been demonstrated in subsequent studies. (24, 25, 26)

The relational schemas involved in working models are likely organized into a hierarchy. According to Baldwin:

A person may have a ***general working model*** of relationships, for instance, to the effect that others tend to be only partially and unpredictably responsive to one's needs. At a more specific level, this expectation will take different forms when considering different role relationships, such as customer or romantic partner. Within romantic relationships, expectations might then vary significantly depending on the specific partner, or the specific situation, or the specific needs being expressed." (27)

Carlita is known at work to be generous with her time, patient with the department personnel she manages and very inclusive in her decision making. If anything, Carlita doesn't take enough credit for her contribution and tends to overemphasize the contribution of others. Her colleagues would be shocked to observe Carlita at home with her own family. She has strong expectations her family will respond when she expresses an opinion or makes a request, and takes any failure to do so very personally. In fact, she is prone to setting up "tests" of their commitment by asking them to be inconvenienced for her and then being injured when they complain.

The highest level of the hierarchy contains very general relational schemas that apply to all relationships. The next level of the hierarchy contains relational schemas that apply to particular kinds of relationships. The lowest level of the hierarchy contains relationship schemas that apply to specific relationships. In fact, several theorists have proposed a hierarchical organization of working models. (28, 29, 30, 31, 32)

Pietromonaco and Barrett note:

"From this perspective, people do not hold a single set of working models of the self and others; rather, they hold a family of models that include, at higher levels, abstract rules or assumptions about attachment relationships and, at lower levels, information about specific relationships and events within relationships. These ideas also imply that working models are not a single entity but are multifaceted representations in which information at one level need not be consistent with information at another level." (33)

A general attachment style indicates a general working model that applies to many relationships. Yet, people also report different styles of attachments to their friends, parents and lovers. (34, 35)

Julie overheard her husband, Stan, talking on the phone to another Tee-ball parent who had recently "flaked" on their agreement to help out at the game. As Julie listened she heard Stan be easy-going and even share a laugh with the other parent. Julie was stunned! As Stan hung up the phone, Julie blurt-ed out, "I can't believe you were so nice to that guy. How come you don't talk to me like that when I make a mistake?" Stan just shrugged, not so sure himself, except that his expectations for people other than his family are far lower. Stan expects other people to flake or be unreliable so he isn't surprised when it happens. In fact, he always has a "Plan B' ready just in case.

This research addresses a question people frequently have about the different attachment styles, because they notice that they may have different responses to (and expectations for) those at work than those they are close to. The truth is, the stakes get higher with more inti-mate connections since we have more to lose if the attachment is bro-ken. We may be anxious about a colleague who no longer responds to us but it will not destabilize our world. However, when a spouse doesn't speak to us for two weeks after conflict it may seriously in-terrupt our world. We might lose sleep or be preoccupied, irritable, weepy, etc.

Adults try to alleviate their anxiety by seeking physical and psycho-logical closeness to their partners.

Mikulincer, Shaver and Pereg have developed a model for this dy-namic. (36) According to the model, when people experience anxiety they try to reduce it by seeking closeness with relationship partners. However, the partners may accept or reject requests for greater close-ness. This leads people to adopt different strategies for reducing anx-iety. People engage in three main strategies to reduce anxiety.

The first strategy is called the *security based* strategy. The diagram below shows the sequence of events in the security based strategy.

Secure Working Model

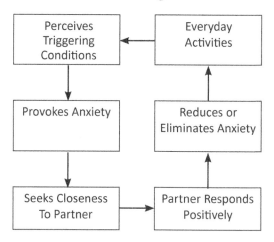

A person perceives something that provokes anxiety. The person tries to reduce the anxiety by seeking physical or psychological closeness to her or his partner. The partner responds positively to the request for closeness, which reaffirms a sense of security and reduces anxiety. The person returns to her or his everyday activities.

George overheard his office mate gossiping at lunch about a possible company merger. Now that George is in his 50's he is far more anxious about his employability, fearful of the ageism his friends reported facing in their own job searches. George knows he could ask his manager about the rumor since they have a strong relationship based on mutual respect. But he finds himself paralyzed due to fear of the answer. When he gets home that evening his wife Joanne sees the tension in his eyes and asks him to talk about it. George was not going to tell her fearing it would worry her, but decided to trust her and tell her about what he overheard. As they talked about his options George could feel his stomach ease and by the end of the conversation they were comparing retirement fantasies! He was prepared to speak to his manager the next day, feeling part of a team with Joanne.

The second strategy is called the *attachment avoidance* strategy. The following diagram shows the sequence of events in the attachment avoidance strategy.

Avoidant Working Model

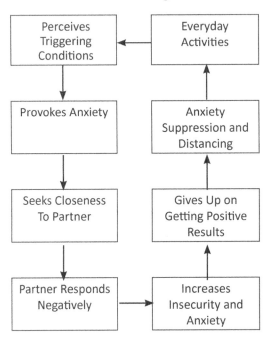

The events begin the same way as the security based strategy. A person perceives something that triggers anxiety, and the person tries to reduce anxiety by seeking physical or psychological closeness to her or his partner. But the partner is either unavailable or rebuffs the request for closeness. The lack of responsiveness fuels insecurity and heightens anxiety. The person gives up on getting a positive response from the partner, suppresses her or his anxiety, and distances from the partner.

Alexia has a tenderness in her breast she is afraid to have checked. Alexia never trusted doctors and fears if this is cancer they will just "chop her up" rather than explore all the options with her. Alexia has been married to her partner Charlotte for 3 years. Alexia loves Charlotte, but knows from past experience that Charlotte doesn't handle emotion very well. It makes her uncomfortable. However, Charlotte notices that Alexia seems preoccupied over dinner, and asks about her day. As Alexia begins to talk about her breast and her fear, Charlotte interrupts her and says, "For God's sake, Alexia, don't be so irresponsible. Just put on your big girl panties and see the doctor." Alexia tries one more time to talk about her distrust of doctors when Charlotte again interrupts her saying, "This is ridiculous. Of course they will tell you all the options – they have to or you can sue them." At this point Alexia nods, drops the topic and continues on with the evening without mentioning the issue again.

The third strategy is called the *hyperactivation strategy,* also called anxiety attachment. The diagram below shows the sequence of events in the hyperactivation strategy.

Anxious Working Model

The events begin the same way. Something provokes anxiety in a person, who then tries to reduce anxiety by seeking physical or psychological closeness to a partner. The partner rejects the request for greater closeness. The lack of responsiveness increases feelings of insecurity and anxiety. The person then gets locked into a cycle with the partner: the person tries to get closer, the partner rejects the request for greater closeness, which leads the person to try even harder to get closer, followed by another rejection from the partner, and so on. The cycle ends only when the situation shifts to a security based strategy (because the partner finally responds positively) or when the person switches to an attachment avoidant strategy (because the person gives up on getting a positive response from the partner).

Brenda is worried about her boyfriend Matt. Matt has been smoking more pot lately in the evening and Brenda is noticing that he is not finishing projects at work and blaming coworkers for it. She notices that he is less communicative in the evening and their sex life is diminishing. It is as though there is Plexiglas between them and Brenda is convinced it is due to the marijuana use. However, since Matt stopped using cocaine 3 years ago, he identifies himself as clean and doesn't see anything wrong with something that is natural and probably helps him with his back pain. In fact, he went out and got a marijuana card for this purpose. Brenda has become obsessed with getting Matt to stop smoking pot. She brings home pamphlets, tells him about websites he should visit, and complains to the rest of the family. More and more she is not seeing her friends and not concentrating at work thinking about Matt's problem. The more she stews, the more he smokes.

Mikulincer, Shaver, and Pereg contend these strategies of regulating attachment anxiety have very different consequences. (37) The security based strategy leads to more positive thoughts, such as more positive explanations of why others behave in a particular way and more positive memories about people and events. More positive thoughts can encourage more creative responses to difficult problems or distressing situations. The attachment avoidance and hyperactivation strategies lead to more negative thoughts and less creativity in handling problems and stressful situations. From this perspective, it benefits people to have partners who are willing and able to respond positively to requests for closeness. So they can use security based strategies to deal with their anxiety.

Attachments and Work activity

Adult work activity can be viewed as functionally parallel to the child's exploration, i.e., a source of actual and perceived competence, just as adult romantic relationships provide the secure base and safe haven aspects of infant attachment. An individual's working characteristics tend to correlate with his/her interpersonal attachment style (38). Avoidant adults tend to approach their work somewhat compulsively, using it to avoid the difficulties and deficiencies they experience in interpersonal relationships. They often report that they would choose success at work over success in love. They give themselves low ratings on job performance and expect similarly low ratings from others. Anxiously attached adults, preoccupied with getting unresolved attachment needs met, often tend to allow interpersonal involvements to interfere with their work. They often report feeling unappreciated by others at work, and are motivated by approval. Securely attached workers report relatively high levels of satisfaction at work and job performance. They are least likely to procrastinate. They place a higher value on relationships than on work, and do not allow work to jeopardize their relationships or their health.

Ginny's family dreads it when she decides to help out by getting a part time job. At first, Ginny is thrilled to share her stories with new people in her life. She feels she is more interesting now that she has something to say at dinner, and tells stories about her coworkers and customers. However, it will not be long before she begins to worry about her job performance, usually because her employer is overlooking something Ginny is contributing. Ginny will get hurt when a coworker takes credit for something Ginny feels she earned. Pretty soon, Ginny will be moody at home, short with the children, and be tearful getting ready for work because she feels devalued by her coworkers. The children usually beg their father to ask her to quit, and Ginny and her husband will start to fight about this. Ginny will feel devalued by her husband because he is so ready to have her not contribute. Once she does quit she will ruminate for months, recounting the various injustices at her last job.

Fear of Intimacy

Defenses formed in childhood often act as a barrier to closeness in adulthood, and that fear of intimacy goes hand-in-hand with loneliness. (39) Other traits or states related to fear of intimacy are high resistance to risk taking, strong need for safety and security, strong need to appear and behave as if emotionally independent, strong fear of getting hurt in an emotional relationship, general belief that marriage is a trap, inability to deal with intense feelings, feeling unlovable, and strong need to defend against financial dependence. (40) Lutwak (41) discusses "counterfeit emotional involvement" where individuals can be together physically yet never take the risk of allowing themselves to be emotionally touched for fear of getting hurt. Two people, both of whom fearful of intimacy, may attract each other and form an unspoken (perhaps unconscious) agreement to have a counterfeit emotional involvement. *One or both of them may even lament that intimacy is missing in the relationship, perhaps blaming the other as emotionally unavailable.*

Greg and Nancy have been together for 15 years, and married for 6 years. Nancy has always felt she had to "drag information out" of Greg and frequently feels shut off from his world. His position is that he doesn't want to talk about work after work, and since he has few friends he doesn't have much else to talk about. Nancy will try to engage him in family concerns and gossip. Greg listens politely but rarely comments. Nancy complains bitterly to both Greg and her friends that she is lonely and resentful. She truly believes his co-workers get the best of Greg and she gets the "leftovers." One night she gives Greg an ultimatum, "therapy or else" and Greg grudgingly agrees to go. Much to Nancy's surprise Greg begins to open up in the therapy sessions and it soon becomes obvious that Greg has a lot to say. Of particular note are issues with Nancy's tendency to gossip that make it scary for him to share what he is thinking and feeling. The therapist's accepting and caring approach encourages Greg to state his feelings, and it works. However, the more Greg shares the more uncomfortable Nancy becomes. She finds herself jealous of the therapist and begins to dread the sessions. After a while she announces she doesn't think it is helping and wants to quit therapy.

This couples dynamic is a common one in Psychotherapy. The more "intimate" partner drags the other one in requesting that the therapist help them with their communication skills and lamenting their lack of intimacy. Yet when the therapist examines the relationship history of the complaining partner they quickly discover this person has NEVER had an intimate relationship. This suggests the possibility that the person complaining is equally disengaged. She's afraid of intimacy and doesn't trust attachment, so she can pick someone else afraid of intimacy and blames them for the lack of connection. She looks and feels more *evolved*, as evidenced by her self-help books, yet she has never actually put her own intimacy skills to the test.

The truth is, if her reluctant partner agreed to more vulnerable communication between them it would likely terrify her! She would be exposed as the one lacking intimacy skills.

Depth of intimate relationships

The attachment figure in adulthood may be described as "a peer who is not a member of the family of origin, with whom there is usually a sexual relationship, and with whom there has been a special relationship for at least 6 months"; and "the person you would be most likely to turn to for comfort, help, advice, love or understanding; the person you'd be most likely to depend on, and who may depend on you for some things; the person you feel closest to right now." (42)

The degree of experienced intimacy with an attachment figure is greater in adults with secure attachment. (43, 44)

The adult exhibits attachment behaviors related to the same components of attachment as the infant: feared loss of the attachment figure, proximity seeking for reassurance and protest at separation. Naturally, the secure adult maintains security in an interpersonal relationship differently than does an infant. The only time an adult expresses external attachments behaviors (i.e. separation anxiety or proximity seeking) with the same intensity as infants or children is when feeling severe distress, such as illness, injury, or emotional upheaval. *When under pressure the anxiously attached adult has an overwhelmingly urgent need to seek proximity in order to feel secure, and a dramatic protest when threatened with separation or loss. Whereas the avoidant attached adult has an overwhelming need to avoid proximity in order to feel secure, and a decided lack of protest when threatened with separation or loss.*

Elaine has thoroughly enjoyed motherhood, and adores her husband Bob. She enjoys their lifestyle and in the process has stopped taking care of herself and participating in the activities she used to enjoy. Most of her conversation with Bob consists of logistics or family business. While she finds it annoying that he hides on the computer after dinner, she is relieved he is home and not "tom catting around" like her alcoholic father used to do. One evening Elaine remembers something she forgot to mention at dinner and walks into Bob's office upstairs unannounced. She is horrified to catch him viewing a very graphic pornography site, which he immediately hides as soon as he sees her. Elaine is devastated and becomes terrified. She finds herself thinking of excuses to stop by Bob's office at work to see if he is really there. She checks the history on the computer, something Bob doesn't know she knows how to do, and realizes he is on adult "chat" sites. She begins to call him 6 to 10 times a day to "check in." She immediately joins a gym and barely eats because she blames herself for his need to "go elsewhere." Bob has a long term history with porn that Elaine doesn't know about. As he watches her pain, he decides to join Sex Addicts Anonymous and get some therapy. He encourages Elaine to attend S-Anon for partners of sex addicts but Elaine finds it almost impossible to believe that the situation can get better. She prepares for Bob's "inevitable" choice to leave the family, just like her father, and becomes depressed. Elaine cannot be comforted by Bob or anyone else.

An adult's skill at benefitting from a secure base or responding as a secure base can be described by Ainsworth et al.'s criteria of maternal sensitivity (45):

Asking for a response includes:

- Clearly signaling the need for support
- Maintaining signals until they are detected
- Openness to the partners response
- Finding comfort in an appropriate response

Responding to a partner includes:

- Detecting the partners implied or implicit requests for secure base support
- Correctly interpreting the request
- Responding appropriately and in a timely manner

Mastering this "call and response" dynamic is the primary goal for much of couples therapy. There are so many ways this dynamic can go awry.

Issues with asking:

When asking for a response we do not clearly signal the need for support, expecting our partner to read our mind or guess our needs.

Some of us might ask once, in a round-about way for our needs to be met and then drop the topic when they aren't immediately addressed.

We could be resistant to our partner's response because we insist on responses being delivered in a very specific way, ignoring all other attempts.

We may lack internal awareness so instead of asking for what we need we ask for what we want and we never feel fully comforted.

Issues with responding:

We may be oblivious to our partner's implied or implicit requests for support due to our preoccupation with our own unmet needs or resentment.

We may notice the need for support, but misinterpret what our partner is asking for leading us to offer something other than what they seek.

Sometimes we respond, but not in a timely manner because we do not understand the urgency of our partner's need.

Attachment implications in relationship selection

The literature on romantic attachment suggests that anxious people seek avoidant people and avoidant people seek anxious people for relationships. Avoidant/avoidant and anxious/anxious pairings are less common. Gottman (46) describes a common dysfunctional pattern among marital couples involving the withdrawn, stonewalling partner (often the male) and the pursuing, angry partner (often the female). Awareness of the different unresolved and unmet early attachment needs of each individual may provide a means of accommodating the otherwise conflict laden interactions between the two. In other words, acceptance of the other comes through *recognizing that he/she is not acting in a deliberately contrary way, but rather following unconscious working models.* Acknowledging the foundations of our behavior can assist us to depersonalize the responses of intimate others and therefore respond less reactively.

Sandy has been waiting all week for the weekend. She feels increasingly overwhelmed by her workload and is craving the chance to "veg out" in front of her favorite television shows. Jim is also looking forward to the weekend because he feels like he is pushing a giant rock uphill all week. He looks forward to accomplishing some of his "to do" list this weekend to experience a sense of accomplishment his current job does not provide. Saturday morning, Jim bounds out of bed attempting to drag Sandy with him, eager to tackle the weeds over-running the backyard. Sandy resists Jim's enthusiastic efforts to get her up and active. She rolls over with her back to him. "Leave me alone," she moans. Jim, hurt that Sandy isn't getting up to "play" with him outside, snaps at her, grabs his clothes and storms out of the bedroom. He refuses Sandy's efforts to engage him later in the day. He says, "Oh, now you don't want me to leave you alone," and heads out to the garage. Sandy is now hurt, confused by what she has "done" and becomes increasingly quiet and withdrawn.

What would help in this situation?

Both Sandy and Jim need to interrupt their distancing behavior enough to ask each other, "What is going on between us?" A frank and honest conversation, without blaming and character assassination, would reveal mutual disappointment with how the day has unfolded. Sharing their expectations and needs for the weekend would reveal that Sandy is not rejecting Jim like his mother always did. Jim would try to engage his depressed mother when he was a child and was frequently rebuffed for being "too much," "too loud" or annoying. Sandy would discover that Jim was not trying to criticize or judge her that morning the way her father did. Her father would frequently be disappointed when Sandy would plan to read or draw in the afternoon, he would withdraw from her and pout for the weekend.

The couple could then "reset" and get back on track for the rest of the weekend. They could recognize what each of them needed and find a way to work it out to mutual benefit.

Holmes (47) suggests extending the concept of internal working models to family scripts patterns that are held in common by the entire family. These family scripts serve to enforce family rules (e.g., dangerous topics are avoided or the authority's power is unquestioned). This theoretical position lends itself well to later family therapy research with alcoholic and addicted families.

CHAPTER FOUR

ATTACHMENT AND ADDICTION AND MENTAL DISORDERS

It is possible to characterize addiction as a consequence of disordered attachment. That is, individuals who experience incomplete, avoidant, or anxious attachment in infancy grow up with an unresolved and unmet attachment need. Some of these individuals will attempt to fill the resulting lack of satisfying intimacy with substitute substances or behaviors (48). **Thus it is the addict's denial of the need for interpersonal relationship with others that leads him to seek gratification in the compulsion.** The addictive attachment in turn becomes a continuing obstacle to those very relationships, completing the self-defeating cycle. And treatment of addiction, as we shall see, requires addressing and correcting the attachment need and its unresolved status. Otherwise when one obsessive-compulsive behavior is overcome, another springs up to take its place. We often refer to this phenomena as "cross-addiction."

Flores (49) discusses attachment implications in the treatment of addictions. It must begin, of course, with abstinence and detachment from the object of addiction. Only then can the individual establish an effective therapeutic alliance with the therapist and/or therapeutic group. Finally, having experienced some degree of security based on the alliance attachment, the individual may be able to explore their inner and outer worlds. By discovering character deficits and acknowledging previously denied attachment needs, they create the opportunity to develop mature conflict resolution and to allow personal intimacy. Flores emphasizes the efficacy of treating addiction in a group setting with an attachment perspective in three primary stages of treatment:

1. Abstinence and detachment from the object of addiction are

required before the individual can make an attachment to group or establish an effective therapeutic alliance.

2. Early in treatment, gratification, support, containment, and cohesion are given priority because these strategies maximally enhance attachment possibilities in the group.

3. Once abstinence and attachment to the recovery process are established, deficits in self and character pathology must be modified. It is essential at this stage of treatment for the patient to develop the capacity for conflict resolution in a non-destructive manner while becoming familiar with mature mutuality and the intricacies that define healthy interdependence and intimacy (p. 70).

Here we see the synthesis model at work: balancing the new interpersonal attachment with detachment from the object of addiction. This results in freedom from both and a healthy adaptive updating of the relevant working models referred to earlier by Bowlby.

Research is beginning to document that individuals with different attachment styles use addictions to achieve different purposes. For example, recent work on alcohol use in general (50) indicates that it serves one of two different motives for a given individual: either to reduce negative affect (e.g., fear, loneliness, shame) or to enhance positive affect (e.g., happiness, inclusion, relaxation). Studies (51) document that adults with an avoidant attachment style drink to enhance positive affect, while those with an anxious attachment style drink to reduce negative affect. Attention to the motivation for addictive behavior may be useful in individualized treatment planning.

Research (52,53) also shows that among people in recovery from addiction, women score significantly higher on shame and depression scales while men score significantly higher on detachment. When addicted subjects were compared with a sample of nondrug-addicted subjects, the addicted subjects scored significantly higher in proneness to shame and significantly lower on proneness to guilt. This suggests resisting the use of confrontational drug treatment strategies that appeal to guilt with the unintended result of reinforcing shame. Also, understanding the difference between men's and women's attachment styles has obvious treatment implications.

Mental Illness as a Consequence of Attachment Disruption

"The denial of trauma and suppression of protest were seen by Bowlby as crucial determinants of neurosis" (54). Modern researchers are seeking correlations between early attachment styles and subsequent psychopathology. There is an explosion of interest in attachment and its relationship to attachment disorder in infancy, trauma, depression, borderline personality disorder, and dissociation.

Lieberman and Pawl (55) identified three major categories of attachment disorder in infancy: nonattachment, disrupted attachment, and anxious attachment. The most devastating disorder, nonattachment, occurs when the infant fails to form an enduring bond with any specific attachment figure (caregiver). Because infants will attach to even the most deficient caregiver, regardless of how emotionally unavailable or abusive, nonattachment is virtually never seen outside of institutionalized settings where caregivers are many and transient. The nonattached child may never be able to form intimate relationships.

Disrupted attachment results from the child's premature and prolonged separation and loss of the attachment figure. The loss is most devastating if it occurs after clear-cut attachment emerges (age 7 months) and before the attachment partnership develops (age 4 to 5 years). Loss or repeated separations may cause long-lasting impairment of the child's capacity to form enduring, trusting bonds. Anxious attachments are, of course very common, 35% to 40% of an ordinary low-risk population (56) and must reach serious depths of disturbance before being considered an attachment disorder.

Whether it be the over-regulation of emotion by avoidant children or the under-regulation of affect by anxious children (57), The result may be serious impairment. Research findings consistently suggest if a child's emotionally dysregulated strategies are allowed to continue unmodified into adulthood they may well manifest as mood disorders or other pathology. For instance, the hyperactivating defenses utilized by anxiously preoccupied individuals are associated with the felt experience of distress, such as depression, anxiety and personality disorders (58, 59, 60, 61). Deactivating (or emotionally restricting) strategies employed by avoidant individuals are associated with more externalized measures of distress, such as eating and conduct disorders as well as hard-drug use (62, 63, 64).

Main and Morgan (65) describe the resemblance between infant behavior in separation situations and dissociative reactions in adults. Dissociation is an anxiety defense strategy, a way of avoiding stress by avoiding conscious awareness, a process whereby specific mental contents (memories, ideas, feelings, perceptions) are lost to conscious awareness and become unavailable to voluntary recall. A recent study by Ogawa et al. (66) documents an increase in dissociation among adolescents with early disorganized or avoidant attachment patterns and a history of early neglect. Seriously insecure attachment creates a dissociated core of the self, an absence of self. It reflects a breach in the boundaries of the self, creating in Peter Fonagy's words "an openness to colonization" by the mental states of other important attachment figures. We have no internal boundary system. Secure attachment requires the early acquisition and acceptance of a healthy self, separated from the world by reasonable boundaries. This is a state of awareness Winnicott (67) refers to as "personalization." Insecure attachments arise when pathological parents force a child to focus on the parent's needs rather than the child's own needs. These children become adults who tend to place their partner's needs of their over their own, effectively abandoning themselves. They feel incomplete, disconnected, and self-conscious.

Submerged

Gasping for air

A vague memory

Of me

Before

CHAPTER FIVE

FAMILY DYNAMICS THAT CREATE DISRUPTED ATTACHMENTS

Family systems theory is a theory of human behavior that views the family as an emotional unit. It is the nature of a family that its members are intensely connected emotionally. Often people feel distant or disconnected from their families, but this is more feeling than fact.

Family members so profoundly affect each other's thoughts, feelings and actions that it often seems as if people are living under the same "emotional skin." People try to get each other's attention, approval and support as they react to each other's needs, expectations and distress. This connectedness and reactivity make the functioning of family members interdependent. This means a change in one person's functioning is followed by changes in the functioning of others. (Think of a mobile – if you touch one part of it, the whole thing moves.) Families differ somewhat in the degree of interdependence but it is always present, even when family members are physically separated by great distances.

Emotional interdependence most likely evolved to promote the cohesiveness and cooperation families require to protect, shelter, and feed their members. Heightened tension can intensify the positive parts of cooperation and this can lead to greater cohesion. However, when family members get anxious the anxiety can escalate by spreading infectiously like a virus among them. As anxiety goes up, the emotional connectedness of family members becomes more stressful than comforting. Eventually one or more members feel overwhelmed, isolated or out of control. **The tragedy of anxiety is that it turns the very attachments protecting us from stress into a major *source* of stress.**

Clinical problems or symptoms usually develop during periods of heightened and prolonged family tension. The level of tension depends on the stress a family encounters, how a family adapts to the stress and on a family's connection with extended family and social networks. *Tension increases the activity of one or more relationship patterns.* Symptoms develop according to which patterns are most active. The higher the tension, the greater the chance symptoms will be severe and several people will be vulnerable to problems such as depression, alcoholism, affairs, or physical illness.

Family Patterns

High Intensity vs. Shutdown/Dissociation

When family members become emotionally overwhelmed and have no way of staying safe, they may shut down or dissociate (freeze/flight). This is an unconscious attempt to protect themselves in much the same way as a circuit breaker flips when high wattage overwhelms a circuit and threatens to cause damage. This alternating pattern of high intensity and numbing becomes a quality that underlies many personal and family dynamics. It is the black and white pattern spoken of so often in addiction circles, the Jekyll/Hyde syndrome that characterizes the alternating worlds of the dysfunctional family system. Swings between high intensity and shutting down or dissociating characterize the trauma response and become central to the operational style of the family. "All or nothing" tends to characterize the family that contains trauma.

Janelle found Allen charming, funny, smart, ambitious, and incredibly handsome when they met at work. He was a sales rep assigned to her company, and she increasingly looked forward to his visits hoping he would stop in around lunch time and ask her out. Sure enough, everything unfolded in the storybook way Janelle had hoped for, and within six months Janelle was on her honeymoon. Janelle and Allen were in their late thirties so decided to start a family right away. Nature cooperated and within a year they had twin girls. During the pregnancy Janelle had noticed a pattern in Allen's behavior. He would be up and positive for about six weeks, and then became sullen, unmotivated and argumentative for several weeks. As the stress increased and the financial demands of a family became more intense, the cycles became more intense. By the time the girls were in preschool, Janelle had trained them how to play and whether or not to even talk based on Allen's mood. Janelle was terrified that Allen was going to hurt the children in a rage, since he had pushed and hit her on occasion. When Allen was tense the entire family shut down.

Over Functioning vs. Under Functioning

In a maladaptive attempt to maintain family balance, some family members over function in order to compensate for the under functioning of others. Over functioning can wear many hats; parentified children may try to take care of younger siblings when parents drop the ball or strive to restore order or dignity when the family is rapidly slipping. Spouses may over function to maintain order and "keep the show on the road" while the unavailable partner falls in and out of normal functioning. Others in the system may freeze like a deer in headlights, unable to get their lives together and make useful choices. The learned helplessness associated with the trauma response, in which one comes to feel that nothing they can do will make a difference, can become an operational style that manifests as under functioning. It is possible the unstable person (along with others in the system) may even over-function at times to make up for periods of under-functioning.

Helen increasingly struggled with her anxiety. When she was younger she would get paralyzed by anxiety, but only in certain situations. As time went on she found herself experiencing panic attacks in historically non-threatening places, like the time she abandoned her shopping cart in Safeway and ran to the car. As a result, Helen was less and less able to attend her children's school functions, terrified she would panic and embarrass herself and the children. This was hard on them, and increasingly Helen's husband Carlos felt responsible to make sure he took time off work to be available for these events. He could feel the resentment inside as he had to return to work after dinner to take care of his unfinished projects. He struggled with feeling "alone" in the marriage, Helen seemed like another child for him to take care of! Helen felt Carlos' disappointment and distance from her, which only increased her anxiety and dread that she would be left alone at some point.

Enmeshment/Disengagement

Enmeshment or fusion (Anxious/ambivalent attachment style) is generally seen as an attempt to ward off feelings of abandonment. It is a relational style that lacks boundaries and discourages differences or disagreement, seeing them not as healthy and natural but disloyal and threatening. Dissension is not well tolerated and disagreement discouraged. The unspoken rule is "don't rock the boat."

Tony immigrated to the US, and has worked all of his life in anticipation of bringing his sons into the family moving business with him. Tony was thrilled by the company's success and proudly told people how one day the company would be run as "a family." Tony became increasingly worried because his oldest son, Pasquale, would become quiet when Tony would talk about the business, and resisted offers to come and "hang out" with his dad at the office. Tony's wife, Sophie, was also worried because she knew Tony had his heart set on Pasquale as the future business owner. Sophie was aware that Pasquale was a talented musician, and she had been approached by Pasquale's voice teacher to consider helping Pasquale apply for music scholarships to good colleges. Sophie had not told Tony about this, afraid of his disappointment. Instead Sophie would tell Pasquale how much she enjoyed his "hobby" because it made him happy, and pointed out that his music would be a good "hobby" to pursue to balance his work and home life as he got older. It was very clear to Pasquale if he went to college at all it would be to study business management and he was expected to use this training to advance the family. After everything his father had sacrificed for the family, upsetting and disappointing him was simply not an option.

Disengagement (Avoidant/dismissive attachment style) is the other side of enmeshment or fusion. Family members see avoiding subjects, people, places and things as the way to avoid pain and keep their inner worlds from erupting. This leads to emotional disengagement. Family members move into their own emotional and psychological orbits and they don't share their inner worlds with each other. This may give rise to covert alliances where a couple of family members ally and form covert bonds. This pattern can lead to the sense that we are roommates leading parallel lives instead of an interdependent.

Daniel and his three brothers have always been rowdy. They were fortunate to have such hardy parents to absorb their various escapades. However, their father Lou, had quite a temper when pushed too far or when he felt his authority was challenged, so the boys were careful to observe that line and not cross it. Their mother, Cindy, was efficient by nature and not particularly nurturing. Cindy would express love by making sure they had clean clothes and food in the house, even if she didn't always feel like preparing it herself. One afternoon the boys came home from school and found their mother crying in the kitchen. They were astonished and frightened. Daniel, as the oldest, instinctively took the lead and tried to engage Cindy. Through her tears she blurted out that their father had been arrested that afternoon for embezzlement and she didn't have enough money for bail so he would not be coming home. The boys were stunned and confused, unsure how to help her. They assured her there must be some mistake and he would be home soon.

The next morning Lou was on the front page with a list of damning evidence that made it pretty clear that he had been caught red-handed. Cindy simply folded the paper in half and left it on the table for the boys to read, never mentioning the article or the evidence again. Cindy quietly attended the trial and ultimately accepted that Lou would be away for the next ten years and she was now a single parent. Cindy never discussed this with the boys, she simply mentioned their father would not be home for a very long time and that 16 year-old Daniel would need to get a part time job after school to help support the family. It was clear to the boys that their job was to mind their own business, do their school work and not cause her any trouble.

Impulsivity vs. Rigidity

When emotional and psychological pain cannot get talked out, it often gets acted out through impulsive behaviors.

Impulsive behavior can lead to chaos when a pain filled inner world surfaces in action. Painful feelings that are too hard to sit with explode into the container of the family and get acted out. Blame, anger, rage, emotional, physical or sexual abuse, collapsing into helplessness, withdrawal or yelling, over or under spending and sexual anorexia or promiscuity are all variations of acting out emotional and psychological pain in dysfunctional ways that create chaos.

Rigidity is an attempt to manage that chaos both inwardly and outwardly. Adults in an addictive/traumatizing family system may tighten up on rules and routines in an attempt to counteract or ward off the feeling of falling apart inwardly or outwardly. And family members may tighten up in their personal styles becoming both controlled and controlling. There is no middle ground where strong feelings can be talked over or even explode momentarily but then be talked through toward some sort of tolerable resolution. Impulsive behavior is a manifestation of high intensity and rigidity is a manifestation of shutting down, clamping down or being physically present but psychically absent, following empty forms and rules. Again, the tendency is to alternate between black and white thinking, feeling and behaving with no shades of gray, reflecting the family's problems with regulation.

Nate had always struggled with his temper, especially when he was drunk. He had been arrested a number of times for drunk and disorderly behavior in public and assault as a result of bar fights. Nate could be violent with his sons as well. While he prided himself on never hitting a woman, he could be brutal with his sons when riled. He was ashamed the next morning when he noticed their black eyes and would vow to himself to not let it happen again. Of course, it always did. This was especially true when he would be angry at his boss and felt powerless to confront him about the unfairness in the workplace. Instead he would drink to "de-stress" and then wind up fighting with his sons.

Nate had a cousin who joined Alcoholic Anonymous and since then his life seemed to have less stress and he seemed to be happier. Desperate to change his life, Nate also joined Alcoholic Anonymous and stopped drinking. However, unlike his cousin, he couldn't seem to shake the stress. So instead of drinking he decided to begin to impose more control over the family in the evening to make sure he would have less aggravation. He was afraid if he let them aggravate him he would drink again. So he began to impose earlier bed times, banish them to their rooms to do their homework and bark at them if they were making too much noise when he was watching T.V. They always had to watch his shows now, because he needed to "let go" of his stress. While the boys were relieved they weren't getting beaten anymore, the atmosphere in the house was only slightly better. In some ways, Nate was worse to live with than before.

Grandiosity vs. Low Self Worth

Feelings of low self worth and shame can plague those within the addicted or overwhelmed family system. Not feeling normal, experiencing themselves as different from other families and hiding the painful truth of family dysfunction can all contribute to family members feeling bad about themselves.

Grandiosity is a common defense against feelings of worthlessness. Feelings of helplessness, frustration, shame and inadequacy get covered up with grandiose schemes and fantasies about what they are "going to do." Family members may not understand how to take baby steps toward success or getting their lives together. Frustrated and disheartened they may take refuge in grandiose ideas of themselves and their plans in life as a way of warding off ever-growing fears that their lives are somewhat unmanageable or they cannot seem to get things to work out for them.

Jerry had always been known as the family dreamer or "Mr. Big Idea." His wife, Patty, had tried to support whatever get-rich-quick scheme Jerry came up with, afraid to disappoint him or face accusations of being selfish and "holding him back." As a result, the family endured regular financial highs and lows. When times were good they moved to a better neighborhood. When Jerry would lose money they would move to poorer one. They moved down far more often than up. This was hard on the children because they were always starting over, having to make new friends and never feeling completely stable. However, they knew the family rule: don't challenge daddy's new plan. Whatever the plan, they were expected to be enthusiastic and listen to their father talk for hours about "when our ship comes in" and his latest plan to "make it big."

Denial vs. Despair

Addicted or traumatized families are often threatened by what they perceive to be the looming destruction of their family as they know it. Their very place in the world is being threatened; the ground beneath them is beginning to move. Denial is a dysfunctional attempt to put a good face on a bad situation. They deny the impact addiction is having on the family system. They deny the presence of the "pink elephant" who is taking up ever increasing amounts of space. Reality gets rewritten as family members attempt to make it less threatening; to cover up their ever growing despair. Family members often collude in this denial and anyone who attempts to spotlight the harsh reality of addiction may be perceived as disloyal. They run in place to keep up appearances (to themselves as well as others) while feeling a sense of despair constantly nipping at their heels. Again we witness the cycles between extremes that so characterize chaotic family systems.

Janet and Al share a tumultuous relationship fueled by alcohol. Al's drinking has become increasingly disruptive to the family. Janet and their three children walk on emotional "egg shells." One evening (after drinking heavily) Al explodes in rage over unwashed dishes. Janet grabs the children and runs to a back bedroom to hide as Al terrorizes them by pounding on the door and screaming threats. Janet locates a cell phone but instead of calling 911 she calls for pizza delivery telling the children that since Daddy is mad they will have a picnic in the bedroom. She engages them in the "picnic" by sending the oldest child out to get the pizza when it is delivered since Al had gone out to the garage to refuel. It never occurred to Janet to leave the house. In fact, she was willing to send the oldest child out to the door rather than face her husband herself. By engaging the children in the "picnic," she teaches them the same denial skills her mother had given her when her own father was abusive.

Caretaking vs. Neglect

Caretaking can be an attempt to attend to, in another person, what needs to be attended to within the self. We unconsciously transfer (displace) our own anxiety or pain onto someone else. Then we set about attending to "their" symptoms rather than to our own. It is a form of care that is motivated by our own unidentified needs (such as anxious or avoidant attachment needs) rather than a genuine awareness of the needs of others. Because this is the case, neglect can be its dark side. We neglect or don't see what is a real need in another person because we can't identify a real need within the self.

Rachel had always had a soft heart. Even as a child she would bring home wounded birds or injured cats, hoping she would be allowed to keep them and nurse them back to health. Most of the time no one really paid attention because her parents were too busy fighting and calling the police on each other. So Rachel could spend hours playing "hospital" with her dolls, taking care of sick animals, and keeping herself company. As she grew older, wounded people were attracted to her and her circle of friends looked more like a caseload. It was natural for Rachel to go to college to be a therapist so she could continue her vicarious nurturing. Rachel met her husband while volunteering at the Veteran's Center when one of the men on the psychiatric ward started paying attention to her and convinced her that, with her love, he would stay sober.

Neglect can take the form of ignoring or not seeing another's humanness. By withholding care, nurturing and attention we shut down the relational behaviors that reflect attunement and connection. Neglect can be particularly difficult to treat because there is no easy behavior to on which to pin wounded feelings. Clients are left feeling as though they have too many needs to meet. They grow mistrustful of deep connection. (Avoidant/dismissive style)

Arlene's mom had always struggled with parenting, becoming overwhelmed by simple dilemmas such as a broken garbage disposal or an overdue bill. Arlene was ashamed of her mom because other people's mothers seemed "more adult" while her mom seemed like such a mess. Arlene's dad was rarely home and Arlene was often left with the task of putting her mom back together again after the latest crisis. Arlene despised her mother's weakness and had no tolerance for signs of weakness in herself. In fact, whenever she felt afraid or confused she would simply tell herself to "stop whining" and "don't be such a half-wit." As an adult, Arleen would tell you she is never afraid. She simply does the next thing in front of her and she has no patience for people who whine and act pathetic and needy.

Abuse vs. Victimization

Emotional, physical and psychological abuse is present all too often in families that contain under-functioning adults and trauma. Abuse is part of the impulsivity that results in families where feelings are acted out rather than talked out. The other side of abuse is victimization. This is a dynamic in which the abused child, having felt helpless and victimized, ultimately becomes the abusing parent. They act out their childhood pain by passing it on just as they experienced it, rather than identifying and feeling their own helplessness and rage at being a victim of abuse. This is how traumatic and addiction fostering familial patterns of relating become multigenerational (transmitted from one generation to the next).

Tamara had watched the violence between her parents all her life until she found a way to move out at 16 years old and move in with her older brother. As she heard her mother cry out and saw her bruises Tamara began to feel contempt for her mother, encouraging her to just "leave the bastard." Her mother never did leave him. Tamara is very sure that she would never put up with anybody's "shit" the way her mother did. She is very alert to signs that she is being disrespected or abused. In fact, the minute anyone she is dating begins to "tell me what to do," Tamara is quick to tell him about himself. If that means slapping or punching him in the chest to "get his attention" then that's what has to be done. Her motto is "stop the bastard in his tracks before he hurts me." If you told Tamara she was violent herself, she would deny it or state that she was only acting in self-defense.

Triangulation

A triangle is a three-person relationship system. It is considered the building block or "molecule" of larger emotional systems because a triangle is the smallest stable relationship system. A two-person system is unstable because it tolerates little tension before involving a third person or even an outside focus such as alcohol or work. A triangle can contain much more tension without involving another person because the tension can shift around the three relationships. If the tension is too high for one triangle to contain, it spreads to a series of "interlocking" triangles.

Spreading the tension can stabilize a system, but nothing gets re-solved. People's actions in a triangle reflect several things: efforts to maintain emotional attachments to important others, reactions to too high intensity in the attachments, and taking sides in the conflicts of others.

Denise has watched her parents fight for years over control in their mar-riage. Her parents seem to be incapable of operating as a team. They are too competitive and distrusting of each other's motives to create a positive plan of action. She is convinced that the only reason they did not divorce was fear of how vicious the other might be in a custody fight! However, Denise has battled a rare blood disorder her whole life. Periodically she becomes very ill and needs to be hospitalized for a few weeks to stabilize her blood count. It was during these periods that her parents would present a united front, both equally invested in their love for Denise. An adult now, Denise visits her parents from time to time but finds if they start to fight over Thanksgiving dinner she begins to feel unwell. It puzzles her because she normally takes good care of herself and is proactive in her own medical care. Yet for some reason when she is with her parents she is prone to illness and, for that brief period of time, the fighting stops.

The idea that a triangle is more stable than a dyad seems paradoxi-cal because a triangle creates an "odd man out," a very difficult po-sition for individuals to tolerate. Anxiety generated by anticipating or being the odd one out is a potent force in triangles (creates an anxious response to potential broken attachments). The patterns in a triangle change with increasing tension. In calm periods, two people are comfortably close "insiders" and the third person is an uncom-fortable "outsider." The insiders actively exclude the outsider and the outsider works to get closer with one of them.

Jennifer is very aware that her sister Laura is her mother's favorite. In fact her mother will admit she prefers Laura's company since she was an easier child. They have more in common than Jennifer and her mother have in common. When Jennifer visits her family she always feels lonely and is unsure about her place in the family. She often jokes that she was adopted. However, Jennifer's father has recently been showing cognitive problems. He has trouble finding his words, his memory is poor and he is afraid to make decisions. It appears to Jennifer that the problem requires a neurological exam but the medical world scares her parents. Jennifer is a nursing instructor and far more comfortable with the language. As a result, Jennifer's mother is calling Jennifer more and her sister Laura is beginning to show signs of irritability and is picking fights with Jennifer over trivial issues. In talking to her sponsor, Jennifer realizes that Laura is afraid of losing her position as the favorite and may even be jealous of Jennifer's new contact with their mother.

At moderate levels of tension, triangles usually have one side in conflict and two sides in harmony. The conflict is not inherent in the relationships but reflects the overall functioning of the triangle. At a high level of tension, the outside position becomes the most desirable. If severe conflict erupts between the insiders, one insider opts for the outside position by getting **the current outsider fighting with the other insider** (an avoidant/dismissive attachment maneuver). If the avoidant insider is successful, he gains the more comfortable position of watching the other two people fight. When the tension and conflict subsides, the outsider (avoidant person) will try to regain an inside position.

Gloria has three children, all of whom would diagnose her as "narcissistic." Their father has survived the long marriage by essentially remaining in the background and saying "yes dear" a great deal. His sons hate this about him, wishing he had a spine. When the oldest son, John, decided to marry a non-Catholic, Gloria went ballistic. She was inconsolable. As the fighting escalated between John and Gloria over that "bimbo," his father became almost completely invisible waiting for the fray to settle down. Once the intensity began to recede, John's father could safely step in to assume the role of "comforter."

Triangles contribute significantly to the development of clinical problems. Getting pushed from an inside to an outside position can trigger a depression or perhaps even a physical illness. Two parents intensely focusing on what is wrong with a child can trigger serious rebellion in the child.

Kevin is the "black sheep" of the family, always the center of family gossip. Kevin's twin, Jaime, did well in school, was a boy scout, and had a nice girlfriend. He played by all the rules. Unfortunately his success made him invisible and the lack of family attention left him feeling alone. Kevin, on the other hand, was a constant screw up. Drugs, continuation high school, multiple rehabs... Kevin's antics served as a lightening rod absorbing most of the family's attention. Increasingly Jaime dreaded family occasions and would find "acceptable" reasons to avoid participating.

Kevin seemed to be on a good streak lately. He'd discharged probation for the first time in 6 years, he was attending school and seemed to be clean and sober. Jaime noticed how instead of the family healing they began to turn their attention to why he, Jaime, was avoiding the family. He started getting more pressured phone calls from his mom, guilting him about his absence on Easter. He started catching disappointed looks from his father when he would visit. Jaime was truly annoyed and puzzled.

The communication solution for stability in the family is direct communication. Relationships are maintained and conflicts are addressed between the two people involved. This means there needs to be emotional trust between family members that creates the safety to be honest with each other, even when it is uncomfortable. Ultimately, we have to trust our attachment to take emotional risks.

Emotional Cut-off

The concept of emotional cutoff describes people managing their unresolved emotional issues with parents, siblings and other family members by reducing or totally cutting off emotional contact with them. Emotional contact can be reduced by people moving away from their families and rarely going home, or it can be reduced by people staying in physical contact with their families but avoiding sensitive issues. Relationships may look "better" if people cutoff to manage them, but the problems are still there and not resolved.

When people cut off family members to reduce the tensions of interactions, they risk making their new relationships too important. For example, the more a man cuts off from his family of origin, the more he looks to his spouse, children and friends to meet his needs. This makes him vulnerable to pressuring them to be certain ways for him, or trying too hard to meet their expectations of him out of fear of losing the relationship. The new relationships are typically smooth at first but the same patterns people are trying to escape eventually reemerge and generate tension. Also, the people who are cut off may try to stabilize their own intimate relationships by creating substitute "families" with social and work relationships.

Susan found her father's criminal history embarrassing and she had never introduced a boyfriend to the family. In fact, when she would meet new people she would lie about her family, describing them as middle class and saying that her father had been a teacher. Susan worked very hard to educate herself and distance herself from the "trailer park mentality" she grew up with. When Susan met her future husband, Dan, she not only told him the revised family history but added that both parents were deceased so she could avoid awkward conversations about family visits. This was more comfortable for her and she wasn't worried since she lived 3000 miles away from her mill town.

Awakening Hope

PART TWO

Our anxiety-based responses to life can include over-reactivity, image management, unrealistic beliefs about our limits, and attempts to control the reality of others to the point where we lose our boundaries, self-esteem, and even our own reality.

CHAPTER SIX

CODEPENDENT BEHAVIORS

Anxious/Ambivalent Codependents

Symptom One: Lack of Attunement with Self

Anxious/ambivalent attached adults struggle when faced with unstructured time. This is because we:

- had our solitude repeatedly interrupted by the demanding needs of our caregiver

- constantly attempt to monitor threats to attachment, and

- were not allowed time to disengage from caretaking

So we became prematurely and compulsively attuned to the demands of others.

Avoiding awareness of our own reality is often an attempt to deny thoughts, desires or intentions that we feel will threaten or contradict the needs of those with whom we feel strong attachment. We instinctively hide feelings and thoughts we assume to be threatening to other people (and might cause them to leave us).

Cathy and Mark have been married five years. A year ago, Mark mentioned he'd always wanted a sailboat. Cathy had no experience with sailing but had always loved the ocean and thought boating might be a fun hobby they could enjoy together. Ten months later, Mark announced he had a chance to buy a racing sailboat from a friend who had docked it at a local harbor. Included in the sale price was the slip space; Mark was overjoyed! He couldn't wait to show Cathy and she was excited with him. She began to fantasize about romantic sails at sunset, intimate dinners at sea...

What Cathy could not have known is that a 30 foot racing boat requires a crew and is designed for racing, not romantic evenings. She soon discovers it takes up to an hour to prepare to sail and that sailing speed depends entirely on the wind and the skill of the person at the helm. This meant that she would find herself "stuck" at sea for several hours at a time, and being at the helm does not allow Mark to participate in the romantic scenarios Cathy had envisioned. In addition, Cathy quickly discovered that people who are serious about sailing and racing form their own culture, and alcohol is a strong component of this culture. Having been raised by an alcoholic father, she was uncomfortable in this setting. Cathy came to realize she found sailing, and the people who sail, boring. She began to miss her old weekend activities and friends.

However, Mark saw Cathy as very much part of the sailing picture. When she would attempt to stay home from trips to the harbor he seemed resentful and frustrated. Soon Cathy found herself fantasizing about the boat sinking in the slip. She began to feel her stomach knot up on Friday morning as she anticipated spending the whole weekend supporting Mark in his passion. She felt powerless and began to feel trapped as she saw Mark move more deeply into racing. Cathy began to worry that Mark would replace her with a woman who was more compatible, and so when Mark offered to get her sailing lessons for her birthday, she quickly agreed. After awhile Cathy began to join the others for afternoon cocktails at the yacht club, and then began to rely on them. Over time, she disappeared into the sailing culture completely, and neither Cathy or Mark could recall her previous reluctance.

Cathy was very aware that establishing separate boundaries and interests was threatening to Mark, and concluded that sacrificing herself would be necessary for the relationship to survive. This conclusion was based on her anxious attachment style formed in her early alcoholic family. Cathy chose a partner who was unable to recognize Cathy's need for a separate personal reality and she devalued her interests. Though she had a healthy spark of rebellion initially, the threat to the relationship proved too frightening to her. Like many of us, Cathy discovered that alcohol is good anesthesia and soon lost memory of her separate self and life.

Secure attachment requires the early acquisition and acceptance of a self with independent boundaries, a sense that I am differentiated from you. Children taught to respect parental needs to the exclusion of their own developmental needs will often continue to play out this working mode of conditional attachment throughout their life. "You will attach to me as long as I meet your needs." In extreme cases this becomes the defense of depersonalization – the sense of estrangement from (or feeling of unreality about) the bodily or mental self. We lack an internal observer, and often cannot recognize ourselves physically, emotionally, intellectually or spiritually. It's as though we have to walk around the world asking others, "Do I look like her?" "Do I sound like him?"

When we lack an accurate internal observer we cannot self-correct and identify our blind spots. We are unable to establish effective boundaries either internally (our thoughts or feelings) or externally (our physical self and our possessions). We are vulnerable to subtle and constant merging with those around us as we take on their emotions and their thoughts. We are vulnerable to the energetic influence of others. Our moods can be impacted and sharply shifted by changes in the people around us. Much like an invisible vapor, we "take in" their energy without being aware we are doing so.

Have you ever felt that a part of you wanted to do something while another part of you did not? Or, you really want to kick a habit of some sort but no matter what you do it feels like some part of you won't let you? Or have you ever found yourself reacting to someone in a surprising way, possibly overreacting to something…just watching yourself react and not being able to stop…and feeling remorse or embarrassment afterwards?

God knows when I was behind my closed door wailing like a banshee in my office, rocking back and forth like an autistic child, I was horrified later by the effect this had on my co-workers. Thank God it was a slow day and not a full office, but I can only imagine what it must have been like to overhear your "leader" sobbing like a madwoman. The fact that I did not die from the shame stands as a tribute to the abundant kindness and compassionate hearts they held for me. They checked in on me and treated me with respect, even when I could not treat myself or my situation with respect. No matter how I promised myself I would "hold it together," I would later dissolve.

In the current neuroscience circles exploring how the brain and mind work, this may be called a frozen or "stuck" neural network. The bottom line here is that most of us have some part, or parts, of self that act or react depending on the particular situation. There is nothing inherently wrong with this…it's natural as we learn to compartmentalize our experience and live our lives. For instance, we change our roles and how we act when we go to work versus when we are at home with our families. We act differently with a store clerk versus a loved one. These are all healthy shifts we make depending on the part of us we need at any given time or in any given situation. For the most part, these are conscious and mindful ways of being and essential to living.

Sometimes, though, these processes begin to act outside of a conscious and/or mindful way of being. When someone cuts you off in traffic and you go into rage rather than annoyance …that is not a conscious or mindful reaction. When your boss calls you into the office and you automatically ask, "What did I do wrong?" and begin to feel like you're about 10 years old…that's not conscious and mindful. When your significant other pays attention to another person and you feel like crying or withdrawing into yourself or you want to leave them to protect yourself…that is not a conscious or mindful reaction.

Our lack of boundaries can be painfully obvious to everyone but us; and since we are so disconnected from our actual agendas, needs, and wants we can feel truly puzzled when someone comments about what they perceive to be our growing lack of self.

Having our emotions acknowledged accurately teaches us an emotional vocabulary we can use to acknowledge and share our emotional reality with others. When we grow up having to monitor and accurately read the emotions of caregivers rather than ourselves, our internal world remains a mystery to us. In fact, our internal world seems "beside the point." This also makes us clueless about our external world since we are oblivious how we effect others.

This is a primary contributor to my own ridiculousness, often barreling through the world completely unaware of the trail I leave behind me unless someone brings it to my attention.

I remember a time shortly after I lost my business. I was talking with a man with gorgeous blue eyes and I had the thought, "I wonder what it would be like to have sex with him." When I went to the restroom afterwards and looked in the mirror, here's what he saw:

- No make-up
- Hair disheveled and shoved back with a hair band
- T-shirt with the neck cut out (because I hate them so close to my chin, which is not good when you have several of them)
- Baggy brown pants
- 50 extra pounds

Essentially, THIS was my regular weekend look. I wouldn't want to have sex with me looking like that, I assure you. I'm quite sure the thought never entered his mind. The truth is, even though I had long since healed up enough to look like a normal person during the week, by the time the weekend came I stopped all self-care and walked around in the world clearly proclaiming, "I don't give a shit about me." My sponsor, doll face that she is, had a good take on the situation, "Well, thank God you're still awake in there!" That was a good point, but for now it will have to be our little secret because no one else would ever know looking at what I was offering.

Symptom Two: Lack of Attunement with Others

Frequently, anxiously attached codependents have not developed an understanding of other people's thoughts and emotions. We can lack empathy for feelings we don't understand. We have difficulty guessing and predicting other people's plans, intentions and motives, despite the fact that we are always monitoring them to figure out how we should act!

Because our caregivers were not emotionally attuned to our developing emotional reality, we never developed a cognitive or emotional "reflective capacity." Since we never had our internal world recognized or mirrored back to us we never learned to pay attention to our own emotional reality. We can't recognize our own feelings nor can we recognize the feelings of others. We are frequently confused by (or oblivious to) emotional worlds of others.

This is a puzzling aspect of Codependency because on the surface we seem so focused on the needs of others. We expend enormous energy anticipating and meeting the needs of those around us. However, we are usually responding to our **PERCEPTIONS** of the needs of those we love, not their actual needs. Quite often we don't even ask the people we're "caring for" about their needs and preferences. This explains the disconnect between our giving and their apparent lack of "gratitude" for our heroic efforts on their behalf!

Monica really enjoyed David's company and looked forward to his phone calls and opportunities to spend time together. Even though others had pointed out that David's availability seemed somewhat limited, and that he was sometimes verbally harsh towards her, Monica stated that she usually laughed off his critical remarks, and chalked up his inconsistency to his work schedule. Over the first few months of their new relationship Monica developed several illnesses and rashes (most unusual for her). She even had one fainting spell.

One night David arrived at midnight, common due to his work schedule, and he began to criticize Monica for being demanding during sex. Monica suddenly burst into tears, which surprised them both because David was not saying anything he had not said previously. She quickly dried her tears, chalked it up to hormones, and continued their sexual encounter. It never occurred to her that David would have preferred not to have sex or that he might be tired. She "assumed" that sex was required of her, and even his attempts to distance her with his "demanding" comments did not deter her. In fact, she seemed oblivious to the fact that she was a very low priority for David, as evidenced by his unwillingness to modify his work schedule to better accommodate her working hours, which were more traditional. Attempts on his part to not come over at all were met by tears and obvious dis-

appointment, which would prompt David to come over despite his fatigue and reluctance.

Assuming Monica does not have an STD, we are struck by her apparent obliviousness to the verbal and non-verbal signals David is sending her. This includes very clear physical signs of ambivalence. Monica assumes that sex was required or desired, but never checks in with David about his true needs and preferences. Apparently David has attempted to state his needs but has been met with crying and reactivity so abandons himself and develops resentment.

As anxiously attached Codependents, we are completely disconnected from our own internal experience, which means we are unable to read the internal experience of others. Despite our hyper-vigilant focus on the changing emotional landscape of those around us, we cannot correctly interpret their feelings. In fact, we usually suspect their emotional changes are somehow prompted by our actions, our inadequacy or our failing. *It is truly amazing how we place ourselves so grandly into the reality of others, yet we feel so insignificant ourselves!*

Pia Mellody, in Facing Codependence, (68) also references this reality distortion. She points out how we sometimes confuse our needs and wants, incorrectly interpreting the problem or applying an incorrect solution. For example, I need a hug but I buy a blouse. The developmental implications of the inability to effectively self-soothe are tremendous. Our inability to connect "the problem" with an appropriate "solution" leads us to various addictions in an attempt to relieve the discomfort and anxiety pervading our relationships. We are uncomfortable in our own skin yet we continually misattribute the source of this discomfort. Deep down, many of us carry a pervasive belief that we are "too broken" to handle or regulate our emotions. We genuinely believe if we ever have to feel the full impact of our emotions, we will die.

Symptom Three: Distrusting the Attachment of others to the Codependent

Individuals who exhibit the anxious/ambivalent style:

- feel others are reluctant to get as close to them as they would like.

- worry their partners do not really love them or do not want to stay with them.

- want their partners to get very close to them while *not offering the same level of disclosure and intimacy*.

Others may perceive this as controlling or even "hostage" taking.

Similarly to the avoidant/dismissive attachment style, people with an anxious/ambivalent attachment style seek less intimacy from our partners and frequently suppress and hide our feelings, suspecting that our feelings and needs might be "overwhelming" or "too much" for our partners to handle.

People who are anxious or preoccupied with attachment suspect that others don't value us as much as we value them, often because we are over-giving and others cannot match our participation level. So, when we notice the discrepancy between our giving levels, and the giving levels of others, we can develop resentments and interpret the imbalance as further proof that we are not "worthy" of being taken care of. It is proof of our foundational unloveability.

Our attempts to seek reassurance of our value and loveability can give us the appearance of neediness, with high levels of intensity due to emotional expressiveness and even impulsivity.

Barbara had recently relocated to the Bay Area and joined a local professional women's group to develop a support system. Soon after joining the organization she noticed there was no system in place to facilitate networking outside of the regular meetings. She approached the board president and offered to head up a social committee to extend the networking beyond the formal luncheons. The board president was thrilled to take Barbara up on her offer and recommended two other women to participate on Barbara's committee. Barbara threw herself into the committee role with energy and focus, and had very high expectations of the other committee members.

Over time Barbara became increasingly frustrated as the other member's were not as responsive to her e-mails and phone calls as she had hoped, and she hosted several social events that were poorly attended. In fact, Barbara did not charge fees for the events, expressing her enthusiasm by being willing to absorb the entertainment expenses for the venues herself! Barbara became increasingly discouraged and even bitter. She began to be sarcastic at the luncheons, attempting to disguise her disappointment with humor. Eventually, Barbara withdrew from the group, interpreting the lack of social response as a statement that she was "not interesting enough" for the other members. "I couldn't even bribe them to spend time with me."

Barbara's reality is based on her assumption that relationships are conditional, but she would be surprised to learn that she sets the conditions herself! She would say, "I don't expect anything of others that I wouldn't do myself." When anxious Codependents begin to earn their attachments, their expectations of receiving an earned "reward" also rise.

Anxiously attached Codependents frequently feel a strong need to "earn" the attachment of others. They distrust the idea that who they are will be enough. We over-extend, over-give, and seem to be always operating from a deficit position. It is as though we are "making up for" everything we are not. We notice other people do not seem to extend this much energy into their relationships and this is puzzling, because for us it's not optional. Over-achieving is "required" to secure attachments from people we love, though we never really trust the attachment because we believe it is based on what we do. If we slip up and fail to "do" our appointed role adequately, we could be replaced by someone who better meets the needs of our partners. It's a chronic stress to believe that you are always one mistake away from being abandoned.

Add to this our **own** conditional giving pattern, which fuels so much of our resentment and feelings of "victimization." We may be so completely unaware of our expectations of those we assist that our anger and resentment can catch us off guard. This is why our martyrdom is so hard on those around us. They know the price we are exacting, even when we are in denial about our own motives and expectations.

If I am completely honest, I'm sure the time and money I "donated" to our business (without my partner's equal participation) was a big part of my distress when he chose someone he had known three months over me. I spent years giving my best Cinderella impression and he chose someone who carried a Princess key chain. Of course, much of my hostility towards her was that she hadn't "paid her dues." She just walked in and took everything without *earning* it. It's so UNFAIR!

Many of us walk around in the world hijacked by the "fairness police." After all, we pay our taxes, don't park in the handicapped space (even at Christmas), try not to burden others with our needs and wants, pay our own way and will even pay yours too if you have less money. We are always earning, earning, earning our value due to complete lack of awareness that **we are enough as we are**. Yet others around us work way less than we do, sacrifice way less, and have more discretionary income due to lack of giving it all away. How does this happen?

When you are secure in your relationships and trust other's attachment to you, it is natural to expect your relationships be mutual. It is uncomfortable for you if they are not. It's weird to let someone give way more to you than you give to them, and visa versa. You want the give and take, over time, to be balanced. You want to be "self-supporting by your own contributions" as we say in recovery, but we also place service and unity in very high regard. If I was secure in my partner's attachment to me I would have divided the work-load more evenly. I would have insisted he cover shifts as well, or hire someone else. I would not have been so quick to volunteer financial assistance I couldn't afford and now tremendously regret. I noticed the imbalance yet did those things anyway because **I expected to**. I even said things to myself like, "Well, he's giving what he can," or "He will be totally stressed out if he has to do this. I'll just take care of it." I couldn't see the grandiose and even patronizing tone in those thoughts. I wonder what it was like being on the receiving end of so much martyrdom?

The misplaced grandiosity is hard to see when you are earning your value. It felt like "love" to be so self-sacrificing and take the burden on myself - giving him a pass to not fully participate as an equal. In fact, I rarely treated people like equals in hindsight – trusting only me to take care of things correctly or to see they were done "right." How can we have such low self-esteem and yet feel like we are the only competent people in the world? I made a magnet one time that said,

Master of the Universe

1-800-I-Know

I thought it was funnier then.

One of the great reliefs in recovery is the opportunity to resign my unofficial role as a deity and join the world around me as an equal partner. Someone who can give and receive. As people frequently note in Al-Anon we can do the "Let Live" part of "Live and Let Live" better than the "Live" part. If we're not controlling your life and monitoring your attachment levels for signs of encroaching competition, what the hell would we think about?

Anxious codependents instinctually resent people who "get away" with acting poorly in a relationship and don't seem to lose the attachment. They have more permission and freedom in their relationships than the codependent. It is confusing and frustrating to work so hard ourselves only to see others "chosen" who have never (in our opinion) earned the continued attachments they enjoy.

The resentment is painful and overwhelming when we perceive that our attempts have failed to secure the loyalty and consistent responsiveness we have tried so hard to earn, yet others seem to just "get it" without effort. We blame ourselves, and sometimes feel victimized by others. This reminds me of the Karpman Drama Triangle, a classic description of the Codependent dilemma.

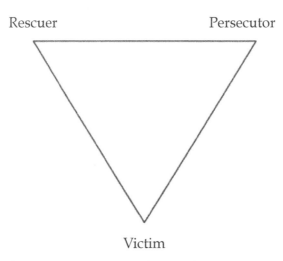

Rescuer   Persecutor

Victim

The anxiously attached codependent will notice that someone to whom they are attached has a "need." Without being asked for help or checking out the reality of the perceived need, the codependent will "offer" a solution to the need. This means we will describe the solution in detail and expect that they will apply the solution we have outlined.

If the person does not take our advice or acknowledge our "solution" we may begin to nag them, criticize them or even persecute them for failing to appreciate our efforts on their behalf.

Eventually, we will see ourselves as victimized by the person's lack of responsiveness to our advice or solution, and may even give ourselves permission to victimize them with tantrums and verbal abuse, while feeling victimized by the person we originally volunteered to help!

Ultimately, we are scared that our abusive behavior will destroy the original attachment, we will feel guilty and then attempt to secure the attachment by volunteering another form of assistance. And so the cycle continues.

Committed codependent's think at least once in their life, "If they would just do what I tell them, everything would be fine." In fact we repeat ourselves quite often. It is not to nag it's because if you don't do what we "suggest" we assume you didn't hear us. Because we know if you heard and understood what we were telling you, you would naturally CHOOSE to take our advice. But don't worry, we'll tell you again... and again, and again.

The painful part of this scenario is the pain we feel when you don't do what we suggest, or don't listen to us. We believe all we have to offer is what we can "do for you" or problems we can "solve," so when our offers are rejected, it goes into the, "See, I'm not worth it after all" pile. We are always finding evidence of this, and we unfortunately tend to gravitate towards people who will provide us with plenty of this kind of dismissive evidence.

Just as badly, we will martyr ourselves by suffering under the weight of a non-reciprocal relationship until some part of us bursts in protest. Suddenly we lose our mind, unleashing all manner of patronizing, name calling nastiness (even death threats) on the "deserving" jerk who has it coming after all we do for him or her! As the final insult rings across the room and we regain consciousness, we are horrified by what has come out of our mouth. After all, we LOVE these people! We quickly move into anxious terror, this time we have gone too far... this time we crossed the line and they will leave us. So, we hunker back down and the martyrdom begins again. It's a terrible cycle.

I was never a yeller myself, so thought I was immune from this type of boundary problem... until one day when I was introduced to e-mail. I'm amazed and shocked by the things I typed to the man I loved all those years. I was off-the-hook! I can remember describing in detail various modes of death for him at my hands, telling him all about himself. It was the perfect tool for a coward. I could "hit and run" and not have to see the expression on his face the way I saw my colleague when I called his idea "asinine." Using flaming e-mails as a weapon is really nasty, and at the time I honestly would have told you I was just telling him how I was feeling. I would never have admitted I was bullying, but I was. I was too busy cataloguing all the wounds he was inflicting on me, and how I wasn't going to take his "crap" anymore!

Lord have mercy on us both. I was such a nut case.

This escalation (or acting out behavior) is so young, isn't it? How old is it to have a tantrum, or tell Mommy "I hate you!" just to wound her? When I look at Codependent behavior I so often see the arrested emotional development that doesn't match our external competence. We are so accomplished in so many ways – so responsible and smart. How is it that such an articulate, accomplished woman is suddenly hurling words across the room, the way a four year old says, "I want a new Mommy!" From the outside, the powerlessness of this approach is obvious. There is no organized problem solving thought in this behavior. No personal responsibility for our choices.

Symptom Four: Escalation to protect attachment

As we learned in the developmental section, anxiously attached Codependents demonstrate the ability to maximize the attention they get from their partner, regardless of whether it is positive or negative (i.e., "I'd rather be screamed at than ignored").

Manipulation is used to keep the inattentive or inconsistent partner involved by alternating dramatic angry demands with needy dependence. When the partner is preoccupied and not paying attention, the anxious Codependent explodes in angry demands and behaviors that cannot be ignored.

The partner either reacts with hostility, punishing the codependent, or with sympathy, rewarding the manipulation. This cycle can develop into patterns of responding to hostility with sweetness and dependency, and responding to sympathy with anger and new demands. The two are enmeshed together in a never-ending cycle of dissatisfaction.

Anxious/Ambivalent Codependents can be emotionally volatile adults who seek reassurance, but find only partial and temporary soothing from contact with the significant people in their lives. Their inability to self-soothe and regulate emotions creates a need for external calming solutions, including vulnerability to substance abuse to address our emotional distress.

Carol and her husband, Bob, owned a business that was facing financial hardship due to the changing economy. Carol recognized Bob was preoccupied by their financial situation and was clearly unavailable emotionally. As time passed, she grew increasingly restless and anxious. She tried to make excuses for his unavailability that would help calm her anxiety. However, they had recently hired a new office assistant for Bob despite their financial situation. Carol observed the new assistant spending extra hours at work, coming in early and staying late as she "got up to speed" on her new duties at the business. In addition to her extra hours, the assistant (referred to as "the bimbo" by Carol) often wore revealing clothing, and Carol increasingly felt despairing and anxious. One afternoon, Carol heard Bob and his assistant laughing in his office and something inside of her snapped. She wrote a detailed and hostile e-mail to Bob outlining her unhappiness with the situation and announced that she would be leaving and joining another company to allow him to have more time with his new assistant. When he approached her to address her concerns, Carol blurted out "Fuck you," and stormed out of the office. At this point Bob retreated from her, and was silent and nonresponsive when he got home that evening, thus increasing the distance that created the original anxiety!

Carol is so blinded by her anxiety and fear of the growing distance with her husband that she cannot see her own participation in creating the outcome she most fears. When anxious codependents become triggered, our frontal lobe decision making often shuts down and our limbic system becomes hijacked by arousal, resulting in a fight, flight, or freeze response. We will discuss this more in the third section, but it's important to keep in mind the adrenalin response to fear often cripples our ability respond from a rational, grown-up perspective. We strike out in ways that ultimately injure others and our relationships, not to mention our self-esteem.

In her book, *Facing Codependence*, Pia Mellody points out the "lack of moderate" is one of the most obvious signs of codependency to others. ***Moderation is essentially a self-containment issue and is related to both boundary and reality issues***. When an individual contains himself with a wall, he tends to shut down and wall others out. In this process, he loses control of being in control of himself and others.

When an individual has no boundaries with which to contain himself he will do whatever he wants to do, disregarding his impact on others. In this process, he might try to control by being out of control and others will have difficulty being rational.

When we are anxiously attached, our inability to trust the intentions and behaviors of others will often lead us to escalate situations and then reject attempts to reassure us. It is a painful and dramatic spiral.

Whether Bob comforts Carol or punishes her, he will have resentment he is unable to voice and may well feel controlled by Carol's outbursts and even bullied into reconnecting with her. Carol doesn't trust that Bob misses her as much as she misses him; doesn't trust that he would seek her out without some form of dramatic statement designed to "make him aware" of her presence.

There is a developmental task in infancy called "object constancy" which allows a child to learn that he/she remains connected to their caretakers even when the caretaker is not physically in their presence. It is a hallmark of secure attachment. Anxiously attached codependents frequently have incomplete maturity in this developmental task, and we truly don't trust the attachment when we perceive there to be a physical or emotional absence. We believe, "out of sight – out of mind." This means strong statements of our presence are needed, which could include stalking behaviors, tantruming, throwing scenes, obsessive calling, hacking into other's e-mail, etc. A moderate response never quite seems enough.

Eileen had been married to Don for almost 12 years, during which time he had struggled with alcoholism and threatened to leave the relationship almost yearly. Don successfully completed an outpatient treatment program two years ago, and things began to stabilize. Eileen began to hope they would have a "normal" marriage. At one point Eileen started to suspect Don had returned to drinking and was hiding evidence, such as bottles. He had become less forthcoming about his activities during the day and since he was working from home while Eileen commuted to work, she had no way to monitor his activities. Eileen began to find opportunities to scroll through Don's phone, read old texts, and recently had started to search through his brief case when he was out of the room.

One night, committed to "catching him in the act", Eileen left the house in her car, and drove down to the end of her own courtyard and parked with the lights off. She sat patiently and after a while saw the cab light in Don's truck come on, but he did not get into the car. Eileen, keeping her lights off, sped into the driveway, threw open the garage door and caught Don with a bottle. "I knew it!" she said. Don just stared at her, and took a drink from the bottle. "Congratulations," he said. In that moment, of the two of them, Eileen was clearly the most frenzied and out of control. Her therapist later asked her, "When you were stalking your own house, what did you think you were going to do if you caught him?" Eileen had not planned on the next step, she just wanted to be right. She wanted to prove she wasn't crazy and get Don to take her pain seriously.

Eileen's frenzied protest was not just a response to Don's return to alcoholism. It also reflected her fear of returning to their previous threats-of-abandonment cycle. It is common for codependents to distrust their perceptions of reality and seek reassurance and confirmation that they are seeing what they are seeing. This is especially challenging when living with an active addict or alcoholic who is compelled by their own denial to minimize and hide the reality of their substance use. It can truly feel like a "cat-and-mouse" game, with a very painful ending. Eileen grew increasingly out of control as she attempted to "manage" what was truly an unmanageable situation over which she was powerless. When anxious, codependents will frequently throw energy at a situation, in a "throw it all against the wall and see what sticks" approach to problem solving.

Avoidant/Dismissive Codependence

Symptom Five: Denial of Dependency or Attachment Needs

John Bowlby pointed out the developmental importance of being able to return to our attachment figure for comfort in the face of perceived threat or discomfort. For avoidant/dismissive codependents, the caregiver was most likely not able or willing to consistently comfort, and may have even been punishing when comfort was requested.

We may have been ridiculed or shamed for requiring reassurance or for having negative emotions about the caregiver. It is possible our caregivers could not tolerate any negative emotions about them or directed towards them, and may have even threatened abandonment— "You could always just go live somewhere else," or "So get a new mommy if you don't like the one you have!"

Some of us may have simply been ignored when expressing our needs, and we became fiercely self-reliant to avoid the pain of neglect or non-responsiveness. Ultimately we become our own secure base, distrusting the capacity of others to provide our needs. We become counter dependent — if I can't provide the need for myself, then I will do without.

We will not risk possible rejection or non-response when asking for help. If we are forced into accepting assistance, we will feel obligated to return to help ten-fold. We assume assistance always comes with strings attached, and we are unwilling to be placed in such a vulnerable position. It is unacceptable to "need" others in any tangible, structural way.

Janice had been in a relationship with Tom for four years when he was asked to be a drummer with a local band. At first, Janice enjoyed attending Tom's performances and was proud of him. As the band became more successful they began to play more frequently and would sometimes travel. Tom was spending increasing amounts of time away from Janice in the evenings and on the weekends. Janice recognized how important this was to Tom, and did not protest his absence or ask him for more balance in his playing schedule. She felt she was being a "good girlfriend" as she increasingly found ways to entertain herself in his absence by spending more time on her hobbies. She began to operate as a single person in the relationship. She withdrew more and more of her energy from Tom, giving him the "space" she assumed he'd prefer. It never occurred to her that he might miss her company or that he might be hurt that she didn't seem to notice or mind his absence. In fact, Janice was shocked when she discovered that Tom had met someone else. She felt betrayed for being such a good sport.

Janice responded to Tom's confession of his new relationship by asking him to stay with a friend, boxing up his belongings, and within three days she had recovered and rearranged the furniture! When Tom came to get his things the house appeared as though he had never lived there. He was "erased" from Janice's environment completely.

Avoidant/dismissive codependents learned early in life that their presence is experienced by the parent as intrusive or demanding, and they quickly adapt with self-sufficiency so as not be such a "bother." Of course Janice would assume that the best thing she could do to be supportive is to "get out of the way" rather than distract Tom from his goals with her needs and wants. It must have been so confusing to see her attempts to please him (by disappearing) so unappreciated, and then to be "rewarded" with betrayal! Because she feels so disposable it is relatively easy for her to react with an "out-of-sight, out-of-mind" behavior.

Roger had met his colleague, Sandra, several times over the last few years at various professional conferences. They struck up a comfortable friendship and clearly enjoyed each other's company. Roger knew Sandra was married, mostly because Sandra was becoming increasingly candid about her frequent loneliness and lack of satisfaction in her marriage. One afternoon, after a couple glasses of wine, Sandra went back to Roger's room, and the two of them had a wonderful evening exploring each other sexually and deepening their connection. In the morning, Roger looked over at the sleeping Sandra, and he felt his heart race. He was panicked. What would happen now? Roger was angry at himself. He had fostered their closeness with almost daily personal phone calls and being Sandra's confidant, yet he had only been comfortable in this role because she was married! As drawn as he was to Sandra, he had the sinking feeling if they ever attempted an "actual" relationship she would quickly tire of him and leave. When Sandra woke up, Roger was already dressed and quickly informed her that his flight had been changed to return home later that morning. While he could see the confusion and hurt in her eyes, he told himself, "It's better this way." He did not return Sandra's calls for the next week.

Obviously, Roger is way more comfortable with the marriage buffer between them and abandons Sandra before he takes the risk of developing a relationship that fails. Roger is more than willing to extend intimacy as long as there is a built-in firewall!

Avoidant/dismissive codependents are often oblivious to the detached messages they give to others, even those they would describe as "intimate" others. While we very much want to be needed (shoring up others' attachment to us), we are constantly on guard to keep anyone, including ourselves, from witnessing any "neediness" or "dependence" we may have in a relationship.

We allow ourselves to love and be loved, but not enough to entrust our security to another or share our position as our own "secure base." Childhood experience taught us that this was not wise and we may feel lonely at times, but are unwilling to trade full participation at every level in order to reduce this loneliness.

Symptom Six: Avoiding Intimacy

When others attempt to penetrate our self-reliance we can exhibit a variety of self-protective mechanisms designed to "appear" intimate without actually being intimate. We participate in the "counterfeit emotional involvement" discussed in the developmental section. With intimacy comes the possibility of "engulfment," being taken hostage by the demands of others. We may have distorted perceptions of the "demands" and obligations placed upon us by those who claim to love us. Trusting love to be unconditional is almost impossible for us and we are always scanning for the unstated subtext or hidden agenda connected to this love

Our fear is that we will allow ourselves to become "dependent" on someone for structure and support, only to experience the abandonment or non-response our "internal working models" tell us is inevitable. We invest a certain amount of "pride" in our ability to maintain our "self-sufficiency." This pride may prevent us from allowing others to give to us. We reject their offers of presents or dinner invitations to avoid the "tab" we expect to pay at a later time.

Terri was visiting her grandmother. She enjoyed her grandmother's company and wondered why her grandmother received very few phone calls. Her grandmother played bridge, and one afternoon one of her bridge friends called and invited Terri and her grandmother for brunch on Sunday. As her

*grandmother hung up the phone she became agitated and uneasy. When
Terri asked about this her grandmother stated, "They just want us to come
over to see their new house so they can show off. If we accept, then I'll be
obligated to have them over and my apartment isn't set up to entertain. I
don't know what they really want." Terri was startled by her grandmother's
perspective and suggested that it was possible that they simply wanted to
have them to brunch because they liked her! Her grandmother "snorted" in
response, wagging her head at Terri's naïveté.*

This leads me to think about Codependents who crave attachment
at one level and avoid intimacy at another. Even when we do connect with others it can feel somewhat unsatisfying due to our lack
of attunement, like one cookie. It is strange how we can appear so
engaged, yet the Plexiglas between us and the other person remains
carefully intact. The vulnerability of being completely emotionally
honest and exposed can be excruciatingly anxiety provoking. It creates anxiety for us when we are exposed and when people around us
are in pain. It is so much more comfortable to be DOING something
(anything) rather than remaining in an exposed feeling state.

Lack of willingness to be vulnerable also prevents us from allowing
others to take care or support us. We anticipate the needs of others
(earning our value) yet frequently leave others no way to express
their love to us by taking care of us. A man who loved me once told
me, "You don't NEED me for anything." And he was right! I never
wanted to give anyone that much power over me. My paranoia, (the
typical paranoia of a particularly avoidant codependent) looms large
when strong emotion comes into play or when others express a desire to get closer to me. What if they find out I am needy? What if I
find out I am needy?

I recently had the chance to challenge this thinking. One Friday, I
had clients booked from 11:00-8:00, with no break. This was a highly
unusual circumstance. When I arrived at the office I realized I had
left my meals at home. So was looking at 8 hours with no food –
which was not a good scenario as I get a little cranky with serious
blood sugar drops, and don't think very clearly. Knowing my first
person was due to arrive in 5 minutes I chose to call a friend who

had the day off. I explained my dilemma and asked him if he had the time to drop by with a Subway sandwich at some point during the day. When I came out of my 1:00 appointment there he sat – subway sandwich and diet coke in hand. Thank God! He was actually pleased to be of help to me. I got a sandwich and a hug and felt loved the rest of the day.

Some of us were raised with caregivers who found our presence intrusive – consuming valuable resources they needed just to cope with themselves or the chaos in their adult relationships. Asking for what we need or want caused them anger or distress, and we quickly learned that the best way to be supportive is to handle our own business and not be a "burden" to those we love. If they did provide what we needed there was always a cost incurred – a tab was due later. Usually, this "tab" included submitting to controlling requirements, demands, or guilt. For this reason, we often chose to simply not have what we needed rather than suffer the guilt or control. As adults, we look for the tab or unspoken agenda even when there is no other agenda. This is why we can appear so suspicious or rejecting of offers with support or assistance.

Symptom Seven: Walls Instead of Boundaries

If our compensating style is one of compulsive anticipation of other's needs, we can appear to be more accessible than we actually are. We are often highly available to others, careful to not "burden" others with our issues. We avoid allowing ourselves to express any need for comfort. After all, people may fail us or be unresponsive. We may even have "Teflon coating," where the disappointments and heartaches of life seem insignificant to us as we persevere in the face of challenges. *It never occurs to us to ask for assistance.*

If we need to have the couch moved we will find a way to move it ourselves. If we are ill we go out to get our own medication and chicken soup, then hole up in our home until we are "fit" to return to the world with our image intact.

Anne Wilson Schaef refers to this as *"impression management,"* where we spend a great deal of energy managing other people's feelings and impressions of us. If we are honest with ourselves, very few people actually "know us" at an intimate level (though they may have the impression they are closer to us than they are). In fact, people who love us would be surprised by how little we trust them or expect them to be available, and how vigilant we are for signs of the impending disloyalty or abandonment. We always have an exit plan ready for the "inevitable" broken attachment. This justifies withholding parts of ourselves and sets the stage for our self-fulfilling abandonment process.

If we have a grandiose streak, we may even begin to believe our own image and see ourselves as super-competent. We may even judge others (albeit silently) for their weakness of getting dependent on others and then "broken" when the relationship is disrupted.

Have you ever judged someone else as "weak" who admitted to needing someone else?

Ginger had been working with Frank for several years at the company. They were hired in the same month, and bonded together for support as they learned the company culture. They had been supporters and colleagues and Frank would have said Ginger was his closest friend. Frank fell in love with a woman in marketing and, against company policy, began a relationship with her that put both of their jobs at risk. Ginger was aghast at Frank's foolishness and could feel herself recoil as he tried to explain his passion for this woman, that he had met someone who truly had his back, someone he could be with for the rest of his life. Ginger internally rolled her eyes and began to lose respect for Frank as he placed himself in an increasingly vulnerable position.

At one point Frank let down his guard and his boss saw him making out in the car with the woman from marketing. Frank and the woman were called in by human resources and fired for unprofessional conduct. As painful as this was, Frank still felt he had come out ahead because he "got the girl." Frank was shocked as Ginger abandoned the friendship, disgusted by Frank's poor priorities, because in her life experience you should never give other people the power to affect your life in such important ways. Frank genuinely thought Ginger cared as much about him as he cared about her and never imagined Ginger could feel at some level that he had chosen the girl in marketing over her – he was willing to abandon Ginger for "love" from Ginger's perspective.

If we knew more about Ginger, we would know that her relationship history includes being extremely careful to never allow her partners to take care of her financially or even to be on the lease at her condominium. When she decides to live with someone they are required to move in with her so that when the relationship ends she will not have her housing situation disrupted. She always knows she can afford expenses on her own. It is hard to buy her gifts because whenever she needs or wants something she simply goes and gets it. It never occurs to her to wait and allow someone else to provide it for her.

Avoidant/dismissive codependents are able to detach from relationships with relative ease. Due to damaged "object constancy," we are quite capable of "out-of-sight-out-of-mind" reactions when co-workers leave or someone dies, which is why we suspect others feel the same way about us! Even though we truly do love the people we are now separated from, those people were never in a position to radically disrupt our lives with their absence. We comfort ourselves with our intact structure and daily routine. This provides the ability for us to act as our own secure base.

There are so many ways to avoid intimacy, and they are worth reviewing here:

Silence – I will not let you into my internal reality. You are required to "guess" what I am feeling and thinking.

This is the "What's wrong? Nothing" game I grew up with. It usually has a backdrop of slammed pots and pans in the kitchen or brooding silence with no communication. If you persist in asking "What's wrong?" long enough you might get, "Well, you should know."

Many of us were raised with the "guess what's wrong with Mom, Dad, Grandma, Uncle, Brother" game that could consume countless hours of anxiety because as good Codependents we want information so we can devise our next strategy. It's a powerful game on the withholding end as silence can be deafening, and if you get really good at this you can ignore everyone around you for weeks. It's a manipulation usually defended by "It's better than saying what I am really thinking or something I'll regret later." However, silence **is** a communication. Ignoring other people or dismissing them as though they don't exist is just as loud a "Screw You" as drawing it on the wall in crayon. Everyone gets the point when being "punished" in this way.

Anger – A wall of anger creates an invisible ring of distance between us and the world around us. People will go out of their way to avoid angry people, even change paths as they walk to avoid the person who "radiates" anger. Codependents can weigh in on either side of this one. We punish others (who obviously deserve it) with rage when they have it coming, yet we are completely cowed at the mere thought that someone doesn't like us or is mad at us. Other people's anger creates enormous anxiety for us by signaling a potential broken attachment. Uh Oh! We will move heaven and earth to manage their anger. It doesn't scare us when we are angry because we KNOW we aren't leaving but we aren't so sure about them.

And aren't there so many ways to demonstrate anger? Some of us are masters at the dismissive disdainful tones, implying we are addressing a moron or someone of low character. Some of us are quick witted and sarcastic – quick to find amusement in the misfortunes of others or small peculiarities about them. Some of us are far more comfortable taking the judgmental/critical path of anger, outlining the mistakes and failures of others in clear detail. Then there are those of us who believe it is our mission in life to "teach" others. We frustrate or confuse them in order to make them "learn" a lesson we feel qualified to teach.

Compartmentalizing – We carefully keep some parts of our life separated from others. We have groups of friends that don't know each other, or anything about our other interests. It's normal to share different aspects of ourselves with others who share similar hobbies or interests. Sometimes we have our work friends, our recovery friends, our friends from high school, our gym club friends, etc. The problem comes in when these aspects of ourselves become secrets that keep parts of us closed off.

For example:

- No one at work knows I am married

- No one in my book club knows my real profession or my name

- My family has never met my drug using friends and doesn't even know they exist.

I begin to have separate lives, whole other personalities and conversations that never over-lap. My partner may know nothing about where I work or what I do. This lack of disclosure and transparency helps us to never be fully available or present in ANY relationship because no one knows all of us. Intimacy becomes impossible at this point.

The internet particularly fosters this trait if you are predisposed to it. You can create entire websites or identities where you can lose yourself in fantasy. Over time some people forget how to come back to "reality," preferring the imagined self to the reality of who they are.

Depression – Depression causes us to lose our ability to focus, concentrate, retain information or have the energy to function at our best. It feels like "walking through mud" and we often will appear numb – not sad – so conversation and connection becomes difficult. Depression can lead us to tolerate situations that truly are intolerable, and convince ourselves nothing will change so "why bother?" Symptoms of depression tend to include unfounded guilt and critical self-talk. We ruminate over things we should or should not have said, worry about other people's feelings about us and lose our ability to see hope for the future. We give up on ourselves, and may even give up on life.

Busyness – Some of us take a perverse pride in lamenting about how we are overwhelmed by to-do lists, endless responsibilities and obligations. Our sense of importance is only matched by our sense of victimization because no one works as hard as we do. Of course, the busyness is usually about other people's needs and demands. We over schedule ourselves and run like a chicken without a head from one activity to another. We grimace as we arrive late to yet another appointment we shoved in between other commitments.

We have no idea our busyness communicates to others how we are unavailable and even self-important. We see ourselves as modest in our over scheduling because so much of it is for other people. It is a wall between us and other people, creating guilt for people around us who may need or want our attention. The people we are doing all of this for may in actuality feel lonely around us, wishing we would just stay home tonight or just get a cup of coffee instead of running around trying to prove our value. Our distorted thinking makes us believe all this activity makes others want us. Without all this activity we would be boring or have nothing to offer. The truth is, with all this busyness we have nothing left to offer.

Passive – We don't initiate or respond in a timely a manner and do not state our preferences or desires. It is very hard to know someone who simply "waits" for direction. Passive people also give the appearance of not caring and not being invested. This happens when we are hesitant to declare our needs and wants, fearing to impose or be "bossy." People have no way to please us or surprise us because we never state our preferences or ask for our needs or wants. We see ourselves as easy-going, or going with the flow, but in reality we are like clear jello or a piece of furniture. We have no enthusiasm for life – no expressions of joy or passion that might possibly be in conflict with the needs and wants of those around us. We are so terrified of conflict we are barely alive.

So we wait, hoping for what we want. Or we "hint" at it, because actually asking for what we want is just way too controlling or bitchy. We try not to takes sides or put people off by being too definite or opinionated. We value our ability to see all sides of an argument. We feel this makes us very fair. What it actually makes us is wallpaper.

Indecisive or confused – We are unwilling to commit to direction or plans, always leaving the window open for another possibility. We take ambivalent stands on opportunities and often let life pass us by due to our fear of commitment or being trapped. The avoidant Codependent wants to know all their options, and always makes sure there is an escape clause. Allowing ourselves to get committed could mean we might have to fully show up, be intimate or even open ourselves to accountability and the expectations of others. We get in a situation where our lives are taken over by the inconvenient and smothering demands of others. Someone will swallow us up and take away all our freedom!!!! Wheeeew. I feel better.

Someone wanting to share our life does not automatically mean that they will control the shit out of us and start micromanaging our lives. We can retain our option to continue our independent interests and growth. We can continue to be a separate person. In fact, when someone wants to marry us it doesn't mean they are wanting to enslave us and spend the rest of our lives bossing us and blocking our life choices. I know this is true because I know actual couples who make it work, and I read about it in books that therapists have to read. But... you go first.

Incompetence – If we consistently perform tasks badly or unpredictably, it becomes impossible to rely on us and people stop having expectations for us. We sit on the sidelines and watch everyone else perform from a safe distance. This is relatively rare for codependents, but we do occasionally hide the full extent of our talents or intelligence to prevent others from feeling threatened or even worse, not liking us. We will sometimes defer action to allow others to step in and feel important, often denying knowing what we know so others can feel good about themselves teaching us something. The one piece of dating advice I remember getting from my Mother was, "Honey, get them to talk about themselves and what they are interested in. Then they will think you are a great conversationalist. They will have a good time and ask you out again."

What happens when we follow this advice? We spend the entire evening monitoring the other person's approval of us. "How am I doing? Do they like me?" We disregard how they sound like a bray-ing jackass, not showing one bit of interest in us the whole evening. In fact, the worst case scenario is Mom's advice works and we are stuck going out with him again! On the other hand, the "Princess" in the tube top came into my business as a terrible listener and con-versationalist, yet quickly got her man. Meanwhile I spent years being screamed at and had my failures pointed out on a daily basis while I was speaking my mind. So maybe the truth is in the middle in that I talked too much and listened too little. Being a know-it-all smarty pants to prove my value is not an intimacy builder either. I think we are back to the mutual sharing situation I talked about earlier or, in school yard terms, "We each take a turn."

Related to this is our tendency to ignore our intuition – our gut-level read on a situation. We let our thinking override our common sense. When a man is rude to the waitress at a restaurant, flips people off when driving in ordinary traffic or tells you what an asshole he is... he is telling you the truth! He is not telling you this because he has low self-esteem which your love will heal. I promise.

I remember talking to a guy who'd been dating a girl less than a month. Already she had gotten drunk and combative enough in one date to trigger a police call. I pointed out that police activity in the first month of dating is a BAD sign. But, she was "hot" and we all know that picking up a random Domestic Violence (DV) charge is well worth it if she's "hot" enough, right? This was an otherwise bright young man with good sense in other areas. But in relation-ships it all seems to vanish, and the voice of reason gets muted. He thought he could control the situation by monitoring her alcohol in-take. Oh, dear.

I remember another guy I was just getting interested in when he told me he had just broken up with someone. Why? Because when he has low self-esteem moments he tells her she could do better and suggests they break up. She went through this 5 times before she stopped taking his calls! My first thought was, "Good you're single." Thankfully, my next thought was, "I hope she stays strong and gets somebody who won't stress her out like that."

Here's another one. Years ago I was completely smitten by a man who finally asked me out. We were walking along the beach as he told me about his insane last partner who was so desperate to find out how he felt about her that she went to see a psychic. He told me that story as though SHE was nuts. What I thought was, "Poor lady. She was so confused about your feelings for her she had to get a psychic to try and figure it out. She couldn't get a straight answer from you." Needless to say, I never knew either. Someone else told me he got married and moved away.

Hysterical over-reacting – Over-reacting trains others to dread the consequences of giving us information or telling us how they really feel. People begin to shield us from parts of their life to avoid having to expend energy calming us down. If they tell us they're upset they will have to stop being upset in order to deal with our "upset" over they're upset! It's just not worth it.

This game is related to the "What's wrong?" game. Only it's the "Don't tell" game. We absolutely don't want to deal with the barrage of words and anger and anxiety we will face if we risk telling the hysterical person our honest reactions to the world around us. We shield them (and ourselves) creating a wider and wider intimacy gap. When a woman tells me, "He never calls when he's running late." I always ask, "What happens when he does?" If she's a yeller, I point out that he has to be yelled at twice then, once on the phone and once when he gets home. If I were him I would just wait until I got home and skip the extra inning. If we ask for something we need or want from our partner, like a date night, and they go off on a rant about how they never do enough for us, we're never satisfied... it becomes easier to join a scrapbooking club or travel with girlfriends. At least we won't have to hear about it later. Unless of course, they whine about having to "do everything" while we are out "gallivanting" at our once a month book club.

Over-reactive people show no sense of proportion. Whether it's a serious physical injury or the printer's out of ink, their level of intensity is the same! I learned skills to manage this type of reactivity because my father was like this. God bless him, he would get agitated over just about anything. "Don't drop that." "Better get under it." "How much is that going to cost?" A scratch on the car or shutting the hatchback too firmly would be a DISASTER! Obviously, this breeds a desire for secrecy and lack of accountability because the consequences (if you admitted something) would be out of proportion to the event. It was way easier to just handle it yourself and not ask for help than listen to it. Doing things that prevent people from becoming anxious (and escalating) became second nature to me. Part of my recovery is to be able to tolerate other's anxiety and discomfort and just let it alone.

Connected to this is all-or-nothing statements such as "you always" or "you never." A sentence that starts this way invites defensiveness, it's inevitable. Listen to your language. Do you tend to use words like "disaster" "horrendous" "horrifying" and other exaggerated terms that ramp up the urgency of your statements? Other people might be disappointed but you are "devastated." Other people might be anxious but you are "terrified." The down side of this communication style is forcing people around you to downplay your concerns and not take you seriously. There is no way to determine if something truly is an emergency or crisis.

I had a co-worker who would sometimes list 3 or 4 things he would have to do during the day, all of which could be done in a couple of hours. He'd declare, "I am overwhelmed, there is NO WAY I can manage this workload today." Of course, he could and did. He was perfectly capable. However, he would spin himself up to this level of distress by 9:30 am! At first I would offer to help. Eventually I just stopped listening and wasn't as responsive when he really DID need my help because I couldn't tell the difference. It was the only way I could survive the constant onslaught of anxiety. I saw my mother do the same thing with my father over the years to manage him. She called it "tuning him out," and needless to say it didn't contribute to a very respectful foundation between them.

Blaming and Criticizing – This is a powerful distancer. We identify who is to blame for every situation but then make sure to tell the person (in detail) about their error or mistake. Some of us are quick to manage our shame over any possible error we might have made by pointing to ways we were caused to make the error in the first place. Identifying who is to blame seems more important than identifying the solution. This is a close cousin to overreaction, because overreaction usually includes blame for whoever is "causing" the overreaction in the first place. This is a shame-based behavior and can be incredibly intimidating. People begin to defer to you to avoid being blamed if they "guess wrong" and so increasingly refuse to take responsibility or make decisions if you will be involved. This leads to the obvious conclusion that everyone else is a moron and if it weren't for you NOTHING would ever get accomplished. And the cycle continues.

This is such a lonely position, as it discourages any true partnership. Partnership requires sharing control and this means TRUST. This is so fundamentally difficult for some of us, and we don't even realize how critical we are. We may actually believe we are "helping" people by pointing out better ways to do things, ways they could be more efficient or save time. We may know we are intimidating at times but believe that if they were competent or "had their shit together" in the first place they wouldn't be intimidated.

Being Judgmental – Pointing out ways others "should" or "must" live their lives keeps our focus completely external. We are so busy monitoring the behavior of others (and hiding our own imperfections) it's impossible to feel safe getting close to us or sharing human frailty. As perfectionists, we truly believe we are in the best position to judge. We may even say things like, "I trust my decisions because I know I have looked at all sides of the problem, so am sure I have made the right decision." The implication of our lack of trust is that others haven't been as thorough. They have likely missed some important factor or data that we have not.

Therefore, as the arbiter of "best" in most situations, we feel justified in pointing out the right way to do things. Our conclusions are based on our exceptional ability to see all angles of a problem and we assume our decision making process is completely objective.

The sad part is we believe our perfection is a positive trait, when it is most likely the feature that pushes people away. It is not possible to get close to people without human frailties. Our humanness bonds us and creates a need for each other. Our dependency as humans is based on our differing thoughts and strengths and talents. Perfection makes us an island. When we are "perfect" no one can contribute to our lives because we have it all together and appear need-less and want-less. It's not a positive trait in the long run. There's a reason "The Church Lady" on Saturday Night Live was probably single, doing the superiority dance all alone.

Being under the influence – Being under the influence guarantees that people will not be able to penetrate our intimacy wall because we are cognitively, emotionally and physically impaired. Any agreements or promises we make are suspect because the substance eventually leaves our body and we may have no memory of the commitment. We are truly not available for intimacy though we might "seem" more emotional. Emotional is not the same as honest, no matter how it may look.

Can Codependent people also be the addict? You bet. The inability to tolerate our emotions or the feelings we suffer from make it common to drown this anxiety with alcohol or drugs. It offers relief from the relentless self-criticism and martyrdom we heap on ourselves. We deserve a little break after all we do for others, right? The doctor is writing the prescription and they know best, right?

Sometimes we use food as a sedative, become workaholics to feel empowered, use chaotic relationships to feel stimulated and needed. There are so many ways to leave the reality of who we are. Staying compulsively busy to be too exhausted to feel. Staying angry and violent to avoid feeling our sadness, despair and pain. Using promiscuity to avoid the feeling of loneliness and alienation we feel when we are alone.

Most of us demonstrate both anxious and avoidant aspects of Codependency since the developmental origins lie in our fundamental distrust of attachment. It is human to desire attachment regardless of our fear of it. When an avoidant codependent allows significant attachment to occur, anxiety and anxious codependent patterns inevitably appear.

CHAPTER SEVEN

A FEW MORE NOTES ABOUT DEVELOPMENTAL TASK COMPLETION OVER THE LIFESPAN

My premise for this text was that early attachment disruption lays the developmental foundation for anxious/ambivalent and avoidant/dismissive codependency. Therefore I have devoted the majority of my research focus to this crucial developmental task. However, Erik Erikson pointed out that development happens throughout the life span, and the Weinhold's suggested in The Codependency Trap (69) that understanding our developmental "gaps" was key to long-term resolution of codependency. I have seen this to be true in my work with recovering clients. I am including an exploration of Erik Erikson's developmental stages, asking you to make the connections between codependent behaviors and developmental interruption.

Development is interrupted by trauma, chronic stress and excessive needs of caregivers. *Why* we have developmental holes is not as important as the fact that the holes are present, and we need to take steps to fill in the gaps where they occur. I often have clients complete a developmental time-line and take a look at areas, or tasks, in which they can see interruptions, and then link them to codependency and addiction. You may find this exercise helpful as well.

Erikson's stages of psychosocial development outline eight stages through which a healthily developing human should pass from infancy to late adulthood. In each stage the person confronts, and hopefully masters, new challenges. Each stage builds on the successful completion of earlier stages. The challenges of stages not successfully completed may be expected to reappear as problems in the future.

Hope: Trust vs. Mistrust (Infants, 0 to 1 year)

- Psychosocial Crisis: Trust vs. Mistrust
- Virtue: Hope

Erikson's first stage centers around the infant's basic needs being met by the parents. The infant depends on the parents, especially the mother, for food, sustenance and comfort. The child's relative understanding of world and society come from the parents and their interaction with the child. If the parents expose the child to warmth, regularity and dependable affection, the infant's view of the world will be one of trust. Should the parents fail to provide a secure environment or not meet the child's basic needs a sense of mistrust will result. *According to Erik Erikson, the major developmental task in infancy is to learn whether or not other people, especially primary caregivers, regularly satisfy basic needs.* If caregivers are consistent sources of food, comfort and affection the infant learns trust (others are dependable and reliable). If caregivers are neglectful, or perhaps even abusive, the infant instead learns mistrust (the world is in an undependable, unpredictable and possibly dangerous place).

Will: Autonomy vs. Shame & Doubt (Toddlers, 2 to 3 years)

- Psychosocial Crisis: Autonomy vs. Shame & Doubt
- Main Question: "Can I do things myself or must I always rely on others?"
- Virtue: Will

As the child gains control over eliminative functions and motor abilities, they begin to explore their surroundings. The parents still provide a strong base of security from which the child can venture out to assert their will. The parents' patience and encouragement help foster autonomy in the child. Highly restrictive parents, however, are more likely to instill a sense of doubt and reluctance to attempt new challenges.

As they gain increased muscular coordination and mobility, toddlers become capable of satisfying some of their own needs. They begin to feed themselves, wash and dress themselves and use the bathroom. *If caregivers encourage self-sufficient behavior, toddlers develop a sense of autonomy, a sense of being able to handle many problems on their own.* But if caregivers demand too much too soon, refuse to let children perform tasks of which they are capable or ridicule early attempts at self-sufficiency, children may instead develop shame and doubt about their ability to handle problems.

Purpose: Initiative vs. Guilt (Preschool, 4 to 6 years)

- Psychosocial Crisis: Initiative vs. Guilt
- Main Question: "Am I good or am I bad?"
- Virtue: Purpose
- Related Elements in Society: ideal prototypes/roles

Initiative adds the quality of undertaking, planning and attacking a task for the sake of being active and on the move. The child is learning to master the world around him, learning basic skills and principles of physics. Things fall down, not up. Round things roll. He learns how to zip and tie, count and speak with ease. At this stage, the child wants to begin and complete his own actions for a purpose. Guilt is a confusing new emotion. He may feel guilty over things that logically should not cause guilt. He may feel guilt when his initiative does not produce desired results.

The development of courage and independence are what set pre-schoolers, ages three to six years, apart from other age groups. Young children in this category face the challenge of initiative versus guilt. As described in Bee and Boyd (70), the child during this stage faces the complexities of planning and developing a sense of judgment. During this stage, the child learns to take initiative and prepare for leadership and goal achievement roles. Activities sought out by a child in this stage may include risk-taking behaviors, such as crossing a street alone or riding a bike without a helmet; both examples involving self-limits. Within instances requiring initiative, the child may also develop negative behaviors. These behaviors are a result of the child developing a sense of frustration for not being able to achieve a goal as planned and may engage in behaviors that seem aggressive, ruthless or overly assertive to parents.

Aggressive behaviors such as throwing objects, hitting or yelling are examples of observable behaviors during this stage. Preschoolers are increasingly able to accomplish tasks on their own and with this growing independence comes many choices about activities to be pursued. Sometimes children take on projects they can readily accomplish, but at other times they undertake projects that are beyond their capabilities or that interfere with other people's plans and activities. *If parents and preschool teachers encourage and support children's efforts, while also helping them make realistic and appropriate choices, children develop initiative, independence in planning and undertaking activities.* But if adults discourage the pursuit of independent activities or dismiss them as silly and bothersome, children develop guilt about their needs and desires.

Competence: Industry vs. Inferiority (Childhood, 7 to 12 years)

- Psychosocial Crisis: Industry vs. Inferiority
- Main Question: "Am I successful or worthless?"
- Virtue: Competence
- Related Elements in Society: division of labor

The aim to bring a productive situation to completion gradually supersedes the whims and wishes of play.

"Children at this age are becoming more aware of themselves as individuals." They work hard at "being responsible, being good and doing it right." They are now more reasonable and able to share and cooperate. Allen and Marotz (71) also list some perceptual cognitive developmental traits specific for this age group: Children understand the concepts of space and time in more logical and practical ways. They are beginning to grasp calendar time and gain a better understanding of cause and effect. At this stage, children are eager to learn and accomplish more complex skills: reading, writing and telling time. They also get to form moral values, recognize cultural and individual differences and are able to manage most of their personal needs and grooming with minimal assistance (72). At this stage, children might express their independence by being disobedient, using back talk and being rebellious.

Erikson viewed the elementary school years as critical for the development of self-confidence. Ideally, elementary school provides many opportunities for children to achieve the recognition of teachers, parents and peers by producing things- drawing pictures, solving addition problems, writing sentences and so on. *If children are encouraged to make and do things and are then praised for their accomplishments, they begin to demonstrate industry by being diligent, persevering at tasks until completed and putting work before pleasure*. If children are instead ridiculed or punished for their efforts or if they find they are incapable of meeting their teachers' and/or parents' expectations, they develop feelings of inferiority about their capabilities.

Fidelity: Identity vs. Role Confusion (Adolescents, 13 to 19 years)

- Psychosocial Crisis: Identity vs. Role Confusion
- Main Question: «Who am I and where am I going?»
- Ego quality: Fidelity
- Related Elements in Society: ideology

The adolescent is newly concerned with how they appear to others. Superego identity is the accrued confidence that the outer sameness and continuity prepared in the future are matched by the sameness and continuity of one's meaning for oneself, as evidenced in the promise of a career. The ability to settle on a school or occupational identity is pleasant. In later stages of Adolescence, the child develops a sense of <u>sexual identity</u>.

As they make the transition from childhood to adulthood, adolescents ponder the roles they will play in the adult world. Initially, they are apt to experience some role confusion - mixed ideas and feelings about the specific ways in which they will fit into society - and may experiment with a variety of behaviors and activities (e.g. tinkering with cars, baby-sitting for neighbors, affiliating with certain political or religious groups). *Eventually, Erikson proposed most adolescents achieve a sense of identity regarding who they are and where their lives are headed.*

Erikson is credited with coining the term "Identity Crisis." Each stage that came before and that follows has its own 'crisis', but even more so now, for this marks the transition from childhood to adulthood. This passage is necessary because "Throughout infancy and childhood, a person forms many identifications. But the need for identity in youth is not met by these." *This turning point in human development seems to be the reconciliation between the person one has come to be and the person society expects one to become.* This emerging sense of self will be established by 'forging' past experiences with anticipations of the future. In relation to the eight life stages as a whole, the fifth stage corresponds to the crossroads.

What is unique about the stage of Identity is that it is a special sort of synthesis of earlier stages and a special sort of anticipation of later ones. Youth has a certain unique quality in a person's life; it is a bridge between childhood and adulthood. Youth is a time of radical change — the body changes accompanying puberty, the ability of the mind to search one's own intentions and the intentions of others, the suddenly sharpened awareness of societal roles for later life.

Adolescents are confronted by the need to re-establish [boundaries] for themselves and to do this in the face of an often potentially hostile world. This is often challenging since commitments are being asked for before particular identity roles have formed. At this point, one is in a state of identity confusion but society normally makes allowances for youth to find themselves, and this state is called "the moratorium."

The problem of adolescence is one of role confusion — a reluctance to commit which may haunt a person into his mature years. *Given the right conditions though, what may emerge is a firm sense of identity, an emotional and deep awareness of who he or she is. Erikson believes these right conditions are essentially having enough space and time, and a psychological moratorium when a person can freely experiment and explore.*

As in other stages, bio-psycho-social forces are at work. No matter how one is raised, one's personal ideologies are now chosen. Often this leads to conflict with adults over religious and political orientations. Another area where teenagers are deciding for themselves is career choice, and frequently parents want to have a decisive say in that role. If society is too insistent the teenager will acquiesce to external wishes, effectively undermining experimentation and, consequently, true self-discovery. Once someone settles on a worldview and vocation, will he or she be able to integrate this aspect of self-definition into a diverse society? According to Erikson, when an adolescent has balanced both perspectives of **"What have I got?" and "What am I going to do with it?" he or she has established their identity**.

Dependent on this stage is the ego quality of *fidelity – the ability to sustain loyalties freely pledged in spite of the inevitable contradictions and confusions of value systems.*

Given that the next stage (Intimacy) is often characterized by marriage, many are tempted to cap off the fifth stage at 20 years of age. However, these age ranges are actually quite fluid, especially for the achievement of identity. It may take many years to become grounded, to identify the object of one's fidelity and to feel that one has "come of age." In the biographies *Young Man Luther* and *Gandhi's Truth*, Erikson determined that their crises ended at ages 25 and 30, respectively.

Erikson does note that the time of identity crisis for persons of genius is frequently prolonged. He further notes that in our industrial society, identity formation tends to be long, because it takes us so long to gain the skills needed for adulthood's tasks in our technological world. So... we do not have an exact time span in which to find ourselves. It doesn't happen automatically at eighteen or at twenty-one. A *very* approximate rule of thumb for our society would put the end somewhere in one's twenties.

Love: Intimacy vs. Isolation (Young Adults, 20 to 34 years)

- Psychosocial Crisis: Intimacy vs. Isolation
- Main Question: "Am I loved and wanted?" or "Shall I share my life with someone or live alone?"
- Virtue: Love
- Related Elements in Society: patterns of cooperation (often marriage)

Body and ego must master organ modes (and other nuclear conflicts) in order to face the fear of ego loss in situations that call for self-abandonment. Avoiding these experiences leads to openness and self-absorption.

The Intimacy vs. Isolation conflict is emphasized around the ages of 20 to 34. At the start of this stage, identity vs. role confusion is coming to an end and it still lingers at the foundation of the stage. Young adults are still eager to blend their identities with friends. They want to fit in. Erikson believes we are sometimes isolated due to fear of intimacy. We are afraid of rejections such as being turned down or partners breaking up with us. We are familiar with pain, and to some of us, rejection is painful; our egos cannot bear the pain. Erikson also argues that "Intimacy has a counterpart: **Distantiation**: *the readiness to isolate and if necessary, to destroy those forces and people whose essence seems dangerous to our own, and whose territory seems to encroach on the extent of one's intimate relations*" (73).

Once people have established their identities, they are ready to make long-term commitments to others. They become capable of forming intimate, reciprocal relationships (e.g. close friendships or marriage) and willingly make the sacrifices and compromises that such relationships require. If people cannot form these intimate relationships (perhaps because of their own needs) a sense of isolation may result.

Care: Generativity vs. Stagnation (Middle Adulthood, 35 to 65 years)

- Psychosocial Crisis: Generativity vs. stagnation

- Main Question: "Will I produce something of real value?"
- Virtue: Care
- Related Elements in Society: parenting, educating or other productive social involvement

Generativity is the concern of establishing and guiding the next generation. Socially-valued work and disciplines are expressions of generativity. Simply having or wanting children does not, in and of itself, achieve generativity.

During middle age the primary developmental task is one of contributing to society and helping to guide future generations. When a person makes a contribution during this period, perhaps by raising a family or working toward the betterment of society, a sense of generativity (productivity and accomplishment) results. In contrast, a person who is self-centered and unable or unwilling to help society move forward develops a feeling of stagnation, a dissatisfaction with their relative lack of productivity.

Central tasks of Middle Adulthood

- Express love through more than sexual contacts.
- Maintain healthy life patterns.
- Develop a sense of unity with mate.
- Help growing and grown children to be responsible adults.
- Relinquish central role in lives of grown children.
- Accept children's mates and friends.
- Create a comfortable home.
- Be proud of accomplishments of self and mate/spouse.
- Reverse roles with aging parents.
- Achieve mature, civic and social responsibility.
- Adjust to physical changes of middle age.
- Use leisure time creatively.
- Love for others.

Wisdom: Ego Integrity vs. Despair (Seniors, 65 years onwards)

- Psychosocial Crisis: Ego Integrity vs. Despair
- Main Question: "Have I lived a full life?"
- Virtue: Wisdom

As we grow older and become senior citizens we tend to slow down our productivity and explore life as a retired person. It is during this time that we contemplate our accomplishments and are able to develop integrity if we see ourselves as leading a successful life. If we see our life as unproductive or feel that we did not accomplish our life goals, we become dissatisfied with life and develop despair, often leading to depression and hopelessness.

The final developmental task is retrospection: people look back on their lives and accomplishments. They develop feelings of contentment and integrity if they believe that they have led a happy, productive life. They may develop a sense of despair if they look back on a life of disappointments and unachieved goals.

Awakening Hope

PART THREE

Ultimately, Codependency is a chronic stress disease which can devastate our immune system and lead to systemic and even life-threatening illness.

CHAPTER EIGHT

CODEPENDENCY AS A CHRONIC STRESS DISORDER

Codependents may encounter other helping professionals, particularly in the medical field, long before being referred for counseling and therapy. Due to the chronic nature of the stress that comes from being vigilant in our relationships, or using our energy to stay unaware of our thoughts, feelings and behaviors, our body begins to develop signs and symptoms to get our attention. The physical consequences of self-neglect will continue to escalate until we finally have to NOTICE that something is out of balance. We head to the chiropractor, the acupuncturist or the chronic pain clinic hoping to stabilize our bodies without addressing the underlying mechanisms that keep our immune systems down and leave us vulnerable.

Attachment Implications in Developing Chronic Stress Disorders

Maunder and Hunter (74) searched the literature on attachment insecurity over the last 35 years and found that attachment insecurity contributes to physical illness. They determined three ways attachment insecurity leads to disease risk: increased susceptibility to stress, increased use of external regulators of affect and altered help-seeking behavior. "The attachment model explains how repeated crucial interactions between infant and caregiver result in lifelong patterns of stress-response, receptivity to social support and vulnerability to illness."

According to a new study published by the American Psychological Association, people who feel insecure about their attachments to others might be at higher risk for cardiovascular problems than those who feel secure in their relationships. "This is the first study to examine adult attachment and a range of specific health conditions," said lead author Lachlan A. McWilliams, PhD, of Acadia University (75). He and a colleague examined data on 5,645 adults age 18 to 60 from the National Comorbidity Survey Replication and found that people who felt insecure in relationships or avoided getting close to others might be at a higher risk of developing several chronic diseases. They found ratings of attachment insecurity were positively associated with a wide range of health problems. "Much of the health research regarding attachment has focused on pain conditions, so we were initially surprised that some of our strongest findings involved conditions related to the cardiovascular system," said McWilliams.

Participants rated themselves on three attachment styles: secure, avoidant, and anxious. Secure attachment refers to feeling able to get close to others and being willing to have others depend on you. Avoidant attachment refers to difficulty getting close to others and trusting others. Anxious attachment refers to the tendency to worry about rejection, feel needy and believe others are reluctant to get close to you.

The participants answered a questionnaire about their histories of arthritis, chronic back or neck problems, frequent or severe headaches, other forms of chronic pain, seasonal allergies, stroke and heart attack. They also disclosed whether a doctor had told them they had heart disease, high blood pressure, asthma, chronic lung disease, diabetes or high blood sugar, ulcers, epilepsy, seizures or cancer. They were also questioned regarding their history of psychological disorders.

After adjusting for demographic variables that could account for the health conditions, the authors found that avoidant attachment was positively associated with conditions defined primarily by pain (e.g. frequent or severe headaches). Anxious attachment was positively associated with a wider range of health conditions, including some defined primarily by pain and several involving the cardiovascular system (e.g. stroke, heart attack or high blood pressure).

The authors also adjusted for lifetime histories of common psychological disorders and found that people with anxious attachments were at a higher risk of chronic pain, stroke, heart attack, high blood pressure and ulcers. "These findings suggest that insecure attachment may be a risk factor for a wide range of health problems, particularly cardiovascular diseases. Longitudinal research on this topic is needed to determine whether insecure attachment predicts the development of cardiovascular disease and the occurrence of cardiovascular events, such as heart attacks," said McWilliams. "The findings also raise the possibility that interventions aimed at improving attachment security could also have positive health outcomes."

Attachment insecurity contributes to physical illness through increased susceptibility to stress. For example, anxious, preoccupied attachment involves a self-perception of vulnerability, which may lead to a lower threshold for activating attachment behavior. In this model of hypochondriasis and somatization, anxiously attached people preoccupied with attachment loss have developed a sense of personal vulnerability and vigilance so intense that normal perception of physiological operations is perceived as a potential threat (76). This means bodily responses and sensations could be interpreted as a sign of increasing distress or a "problem." Another example is that avoidant attachment involves an attitude of heightened interpersonal distrust, such that situations requiring intimacy or interdependence (including a situation of apparent "social support") may be perceived as threatening.

Attachment insecurity contributes to physical illness through increasing the intensity or duration of the physiological stress response. For example, Sroufe and Waters (77) measured changes in heart rate in children during the Strange Situation. Heart rate **acceleration** reflects an aversive or defensive response, and heart rate **deceleration** reflects attention to the stimulus. The study reported that all children show heart-rate increases during separation, which remain elevated until reunion with the parent. At reunion, secure infants exhibit a soothing calm, returning to their baseline heart rate in less than a minute. Both ambivalent and avoidant children exhibit elevations of heart rate much longer into the reunion sequence, experiencing greater stress. Ambivalent infants request to be put down before their heart rates recovered to the pre-separation level. Then after being put down, with their heart rates still elevated, they reach up to be held again. Avoidant children show an increased heart rate from the beginning of separation until long into the reunion, *despite the fact that they display very little distress*. These stress response patterns become habitual and eventually account for susceptibility to physical illness.

Attachment insecurity contributes to physical illness through decreased stress buffering through social support. Secure individuals perceive more available support and seek out that support more at times of stress than avoidant or ambivalent (preoccupied) individuals (78, 79, 80). Social support is widely considered to be beneficial to a range of health outcomes (81). Perceiving support as threatening or nonexistent endangers one's health.

Attachment insecurity contributes to physical illness through increased use of external regulators of affect. Since insecure attachment results in deficits in internal affect regulation (82, 83), insecurity is associated with greater use of external regulators. A number of behavioral strategies that are used to regulate dysphoric affect (to soothe, to distract or to excite) are also risk factors for disease, including smoking tobacco, drinking alcohol, using other psychoactive drugs, over-eating, under-eating and engaging in risky sexual activity. For example, adults with avoidant attachment drink alcohol to enhance positive affect (84). External regulation of negative emotions through food intake has been shown to be a mechanism responsible for obesity (85). Also, attachment style has a strong influence on sexual behavior (86). So any tendency to use substances or external behaviors to reduce stress constitute an increased risk for physical illness.

Finally, attachment insecurity contributes to physical illness through the failure or nonuse of protective factors such as social support, treatment adherence and symptom reporting. In the absence of positive body image, sensitivity to bodily needs or sense of self-control (products of secure attachment) health crises may produce defensiveness and especially denial. Denial of physical condition and needs during a health crisis can defer benefits from supportive resources, increasing risk. Two studies directly support the link between attachment insecurity and symptom reporting. Avoidant attachment individuals tend to report symptoms less often, relying on emotional self-control instead (87). Anxious and preoccupied individuals tend to report an excess of medically unexplained symptoms compared with securely attached individuals with the same disease (88, 89).

Abuse or neglect in childhood contributes to increased risk in adulthood for terminal disease. Felitti et al. (90) found a strong relationship between exposure to abuse or household dysfunction during childhood and several of the leading causes of death in adults. Seven categories of adverse childhood experiences were studied: psychological, physical or sexual abuse; violence against the mother; living with substance abusers, the mentally ill or suicidal or even imprisoned. The health risk factors were: heart disease, cancer, chronic lung disease, skeletal fractures and liver disease. Persons who had experienced four or more categories of childhood exposure, compared to those who had experienced none, *had four-fold to twelve-fold increased health risks for alcoholism, drug abuse, depression, and suicide attempts.*

Chapter Nine

Physiology of the Stress Response Connected to Codependency

My experience of separation from such an enmeshed relationship was physically painful. My body was chronically sore from stiffening and clenching in an attempt to not cry at inopportune times (like in the classroom). My chest was always tight and I frequently had a hard time catching my breath which I experienced frequently in the classroom or in the late evening. I had surges of anxiety throughout the day, so would feel myself get warm and even noticed an occasional tremor as the adrenalin coursed through me. In fact, every time I had the thought, "This is too hard. I can't do it," when thinking about our broken attachment my heart would race. This happened throughout the day, all day, and I was exhausted. My adrenal system was working overtime, and my hormonal system shut down so that my monthly cycle stopped for months. I learned how physically painful grief could be.

Understanding the nervous system response to stress is important in explaining the stress-related diseases and conditions created by the chronic stress of codependency. While attachment issues set the emotional and developmental stage for future behaviors, the fight, flight or freeze response is the physical mechanism that leads to our physical deterioration and lowered immune system. The fight, flight or freeze response prepares us to respond to an emergency.

The Alarm Reaction

The human body and human mind each have a set of very important and very predictable responses to threat. Threat may come from an external source such as an attacker or an internal source such as fear of abandonment (as is the case with Codependency).

One common reaction to danger or threat has been labeled the "fight or flight" reaction. In the initial stages of this reaction, there is a response called the *alarm reaction*

Alarm Reaction

Think about what happens when you feel threatened. Your racing heart, sweaty palms, nausea and sense of impending harm are all symptomatic of this alarm reaction.

During the traumatic event, all aspects of the individual's functioning change including feeling, thinking and behaving. For instance, someone under direct assault abandons thoughts of the future or abstract plans for survival. At that exact moment, all of the victim's thinking, behaving and feeling is directed by more primitive parts of the brain.

A frightened child in a threatening situation doesn't focus on the words being spoken or yelled; instead, he or she is busy attending to the threat-related signals in their environment.

The fearful child will key in to nonverbal signs of communication, cues such as:

- eye contact
- facial expression
- body posture
- proximity to the threat

The internal state of the child also shifts with the level of perceived threat. With increased threat, a child moves along the arousal continuum from vigilance to terror.

The Arousal Continuum

The arousal continuum is characterized by many physiological changes. Under threat, the sympathetic nervous system increases each of these functions in a gradual fashion:

- heart rate
- blood pressure
- respiration
- glucose stored in muscle is released to prepare the large skeletal muscles of your arms and legs for either a fight or a flight

These changes in the central nervous system cause *hypervigilance*. Under threat, the child tunes out all non-critical information. These actions prepare the child to do battle or run away from the potential threat.

Dissociation (Freeze)

The fight-or-flight response is a well-characterized reaction to danger as we've already discussed. A second common reaction pattern to threat is *dissociation*. Dissociation is the mental mechanism by which one withdraws attention from the outside world and focuses on the inner world.

Because of their small size and limited physical capabilities, young children do not usually have the fight-or-flight option in a threatening situation. When fighting or physically fleeing is not possible, the child may use avoidant and psychological fleeing mechanisms that are categorized as *dissociative*.

Dissociation due to threat and/or trauma may involve:

- a distorted sense of time
- a detached feeling that you are observing something happening to you as if it is unreal -- the sense that you may be watching a movie of your life
- in extreme cases, children may withdraw into an elaborate fantasy world where they may assume special powers or strengths

Like the alarm response, this "defeat" or dissociative response happens along a continuum. The intensity of the dissociation varies with the intensity and duration of the traumatic event. Remember, even when we're not threatened we use dissociative mental mechanisms (such as daydreaming) all the time. During a traumatic event all children and most adults use some degree of dissociation, the sense that you are watching yourself, for example. However, some individuals will use dissociation is a primary adaptive response.

For most children and adults the adaptive response to an acute trauma involves a mixture of hyperarousal and dissociation. During the actual trauma, the child feels threatened and the arousal systems will activate. As the threat increases, the child moves along the arousal continuum. At some point along this continuum the dissociative response is activated and a host of protective mental (decreased perception of anxiety and pain) and physiological (decreased heart rate) responses occur. The hyperarousal system begins to slow down.

Today we know the body cannot tell the difference between an emotional emergency and physical danger. When triggered, it will respond to either situation by pumping out stress chemicals designed to facilitate fight or flight. In the case of childhood problems, where the family itself has become the source of significant stress, there may be no opportunity to fight or flee. For many children, the only perceived option is to freeze and shut down their inner responses by numbing or withdrawing into a fantasy world.

When young children get frightened and go into fight, flight or freeze they have no way of interpreting the level of threat or using reason to modulate or understand what is happening. The brain's limbic system becomes frozen in a fear response. The only way out is for a caring adult to hold, reassure and restore the child to a state of equilibrium which is available if a **secure attachment** with the caregiver exists. When primary caregivers are not available to soothe and reassure, the child is left to the fight, flight or freeze system without support.

Why is the Fight or Flight Response Important?

Understanding the sympathetic and parasympathetic nervous system response to stress is important in explaining the stress-related diseases and conditions created by the chronic stress of codependency. While attachment issues set the emotional and developmental stage for future behaviors, the fight or flight response is the physical mechanism that leads to our physiological deterioration and lowered immune system. The fight or flight response (named by Cannon and Selye in the 1930s) is a pattern of physiological responses that prepare us to respond to an emergency.

In the animal kingdom the rules of survival are simple: only the stronger survives. When faced with danger, the two main options are fighting (when you perceive the enemy to be weaker or when defending your cubs or herd) and running away (when you encounter a huge hungry lion, for example). In the face of danger the body shifts its inner-balance to high physiological arousal which enables fight or flight. It is designed as a short-term response to threat and the level of arousal is supposed to settle within a short period of time – after the lion is gone.

Let's emphasize two points about this healthy stress response. First, it takes priority over all other metabolic functions. Second, it wasn't designed to last very long.

So, how is fighting a lion related to anxiety about an upcoming meeting with our employer? Our physical response to a perceived threat is EXACTLY the same. When our attachment issues are triggered we physically respond just as though it was a lion. But lions only visit occasionally, whereas we perceive threats to our attachment frequently; up to several times a day. Each time, we experience intense adrenal system arousal and release cortisol (the "rust" of the human body). We'll look at this in greater depth later.

First, we look at how the Autonomic Nervous System (ANS) responds to threat and how that translates into physical damage over time. The ANS is composed of the sympathetic and parasympathetic systems. The ANS affects many bodily functions instantly and directly while hormones have slower yet wider effect on the body. Both hormones and neurons communicate with cells and create the delicate dynamic balance between the body and its surroundings through paired systems and feedback mechanisms.

The ANS is responsible for many functions in the body that occur "automatically" such as digestion, heart rate, blood pressure and body temperature. The activity of the autonomic nervous system takes place beneath our conscious control. It is automatic.

There are two branches of the ANS that are designed to regulate the fight-or-flight response on a constant basis. The *sympathetic nervous system* is the part of the ANS that is responsible for initiating the fight-or-flight response. Each time we have a thought of danger or pain, the sympathetic nervous system initiates the fight-or-flight response to prepare us to handle the potential danger or pain. It is an automatic reaction. *We only need to think that we are in danger* and the flood of physiological and emotional activity is turned on and goes into perfect functioning to increase power, speed and strength. This is key because it means that you don't have to actually threaten to leave me. I can just picture you leaving me and fully stimulate this response.

The other branch of the ANS is called the *parasympathetic nervous system*. This branch of nervous activity is designed to return the physiology to a state of *homeostasis,* or balance, after the threat is no longer perceived to be imminent. Homeostasis is a state of internal stability of our physiology and our emotions. In other words, the function of the parasympathetic nervous system is to slow things down and return us to a calmer state. During parasympathetic activity, blood concentrates in the central organs for such processes as digestion and storage of energy reserves. Breathing is slow, as is the heart rate. Blood pressure and body temperature drop. In general, muscle tension decreases. During parasympathetic activity (general relaxation) we are quiet and calm. The body regenerates and restores for future activity.

The autonomic nervous system is controlled by the *hypothalamus*, which is commonly known as the "master gland." The hypothalamus receives the message of danger from the higher-order thinking component of the mind and delivers a message through the nervous system that connects directly to every other system of the body. The hypothalamus also delivers a message to the endocrine system to initiate the secretion of hormones. **The hormones, primarily adrenalin (epinephrine) and cortisol**, flood the bloodstream and travel throughout the body delivering information to cells and systems which make us speedier and more powerful.

Parasympathetic response systems do not help us operate at high capacity to escape from a lion. Therefore their work is suppressed in order to divert energy to those vital systems involved in increasing speed and power. For example, you don't need the immune system or your reproductive system to help you escape from the lion.

What does the fight or flight response look like in the moment?

In the moment of feeling threatened, immediate and significant changes occur in our bodies, including: increased heart rate, blood pressure and respiration. This pumps more blood around the body supplying more oxygen to the muscles and heart-lung system.

Also, sugar rates in the blood increase, allowing rapid energy use and accelerating metabolism for emergency actions.

Blood thickens to increase oxygen supply (red cells), to enable better defense from infections (white cells) and to stop bleeding quickly (platelets). Senses sharpen. The pupils dilate; hearing is better etc., allowing rapid responses.

The body prioritizes blood flow, increasing blood supply to peripheral muscles and the heart as well as motor and basic-function regions in the brain. Whereas blood flow is decreased to the digestive system and irrelevant brain regions (such as speech areas – making it hard to find our words). This also causes secretion of body wastes, leaving the body lighter.

There occurs heightened secretion of adrenaline and other stress hormones to further increase the response, and to strengthen relevant systems.

Secretion of endorphins also increases. Endorphins are natural painkillers, providing an instant defense against pain.

There are further systems involved in the fight or flight response and even more consequences to it. It is clear that the fight or flight response is crucial to dealing with some short-term dangers but is incapable of dealing with long-term stress. Any return to homeostasis is always interrupted and access to parasympathetic responses, like our immune system, is suppressed. The grave consequences of long-term stress on our body and mind are a direct result of this suppression, and the over activation of adrenalin systems often leads to adrenal fatigue and chronic illness.

Adrenaline is by far the most important single hormone regarding stress, playing a major role in the stress reaction. The action of the adrenal system is so significant, I'm devoting an entire chapter to it.

CHAPTER TEN

STRESS AND THE ADRENAL GLANDS

Unlike our ancestors, we live with constant stress. Instead of occasional, acute demands followed by rest, we're constantly overworked, undernourished, exposed to environmental toxins and worrying about others — with no let-up.

Every challenge to the mind and body creates a demand on the adrenal glands. And the list of challenges is endless: lack of sleep, a demanding boss, the threat of losing your job, financial pressures, personality conflicts, yo-yo dieting, relationship turmoil, death or illness of a loved one, skipping meals, reliance on stimulants like caffeine and carbs, digestive problems, over-exercise, illness or infection, unresolved emotional issues from our past or present, and more. The result is adrenal glands that are constantly on high alert.

The Destructive Effect of High Cortisol Levels

What is cortisol? In its normal function, cortisol helps us meet these challenges by converting proteins into energy, releasing glycogen, and counteracting inflammation. For a short time, that's okay. But at sustained high levels, cortisol gradually tears your body down.

Sustained high cortisol levels...

- destroy healthy muscle and bone.
- slow down healing and normal cell regeneration.
- co-opt biochemicals needed to make other vital hormones.
- impair digestion, metabolism and mental function.
- interfere with healthy endocrine function.
- weaken your immune system.

Adrenal fatigue may be a factor in many conditions, including fibro-myalgia, hypothyroidism, chronic fatigue syndrome, arthritis and more. It can also be associated with a host of unpleasant signs and symptoms from acne to hair loss.

The Loss of DHEA Production

DHEA (*dehydroepiandrosterone*) is an immediate precursor hormone to estrogen, progesterone, and testosterone. When the adrenals are chronically overworked and straining to maintain high cortisol levels they lose the capacity to produce DHEA in sufficient amounts. When DHEA is in short supply, people have a hard time balancing their hormones.

This happens because Mother Nature will always favor survival (our adrenals' primary function) over reproduction (our adrenal's secondary function). That's why hormonal balance becomes increasingly problematic as stressed-out women approach midlife. It's bad enough that ovarian sex hormone production declines naturally, when you throw stress on top of that you can see how vulnerable we are to illness.

Over time low DHEA leads to fatigue, bone loss, loss of muscle mass, depression, aching joints, decreased sex drive, and impaired immune function. All these symptoms we look for Hormone Replacement Therapy to replace. Stress masquerading as peri-menopause? It's not "the change" but rather the lack of change we suffer from.

Adrenal Fatigue

Do these symptoms sound familiar? Are you feeling fatigue, insomnia, weight gain and depression? If so, your underlying problem could be adrenal fatigue.

Are your adrenals imbalanced?

Here are some questions to help you check how much strain you may be placing on your adrenal system.

- Are you always on the run?

- Do you feel like you "can never do enough?"
- Does everything seem like it's a whole lot harder for you than it should be?
- Do you find it difficult to get out of bed in the morning?
- Do you use caffeine or sugar to bolster your flagging energy in the afternoon?
- Do you feel weary and irritable much of the time?
- Do you often crave salty foods or binge on sugar?
- Do you fall asleep while reading or while watching movies?
- Do you struggle to "come down" at night so you can get to sleep?

If the answer to more than one of these questions is yes, you may consider talking to a functional medicine practitioner about your adrenal glands.

After the break-up of my business partnership I felt "bone-weary." It was impossible to concentrate, and I felt as though there was no extra energy to draw upon. Now I understand the phrase "grief stricken," which translates in my experience to feeling paralyzed or frozen at times. The simplest concentration tasks exhausted me. I felt irritated easily. I found myself snapping at people when they'd ask things of me. They had no idea how little energy I had to spare. The depression and desire to sleep haunted me all the time, which for an "energizer bunny" type like me was very painful. I knew that caffeine was a bad idea but did it anyway. On the plus side, I did drink more water during this time which seemed to help but I still showed symptoms of dehydration, mostly from doing so much crying. I was new to this level of pain and frequency of tears. It was a great relief to finally know what was happening to me, that I was experiencing the result of the intense adrenal surges I had been having for weeks. Now, I could get into solution for a change and begin moving toward physical healing.

Anyone with these symptoms can get an adrenal fatigue test which assesses cortisol levels. Thousands of people with these symptoms have taken the adrenal fatigue test, and the results: only 10–15% have cortisol levels indicating healthy adrenal function, 85–90% suffer impaired function ranging from significant adrenal stress to complete adrenal exhaustion.

The effects of adrenal dysfunction can be profound: fatigue and weakness, suppression of the immune system, muscle and bone loss, moodiness or depression, hormonal imbalance, skin problems, autoimmune disorders and dozens of other symptoms and health concerns. Be on the lookout! And get tested if you feel you are suffering.

Natural Adrenal Support — How to Restore Healthy Adrenal Function

The first step is a full physical exam. Make certain there are no serious underlying medical issues causing your symptoms. People with mild to moderate adrenal fatigue can see significant improvement through these simple steps:

- *Enrich your nutrition, reduce carbohydrates, and cut back on stimulants.*

- *Consider nutritional supplements that support adrenal function.* Start with a high-quality multivitamin–mineral complex rich in stress vitamins, minerals, and essential fatty acids. Talk to an herbalist or naturopath to learn how select herbs help restore adrenal balance, and find the best combination of herbs for you.

Adrenal draining	Adrenal restoring
• Drinks that contain caffeine	• Ginseng • Eleuthero/Siberian ginseng (in the morning)
• Alcohol	• Herbal teas like chamomile, passionflower, valerian
• Gatorade	• Vegetable juice (with salt), like V-8

- *Reduce stress, include moderate exercise and take more time for yourself.* It's helpful to make a list of your stressors, especially those that are ongoing or self-imposed.

- *Get more rest.* Your body needs time to heal!

People with more entrenched symptoms or those who have reached complete adrenal exhaustion may need further intervention. Finally, we can never underestimate the power of perceived stress. Guilt, pain from past hurts, self-destructive habits and unresolved relationship problems may be functioning as ever-present stressors in your life. **Dealing directly with these problems is far more beneficial than spending a lifetime compensating for the stress they create.**

In all but the most extreme cases, you can expect to see dramatic improvement in four to six months. For mild to moderate adrenal fatigue, the turnaround can be faster. Know this: you may feel you're just too tired to make changes now. But by moving forward in incremental stages you'll build the strength you need to stay with it and you will love how you feel when you do!

There

I'm still in there

Ridiculous

Awake

Alive

CHAPTER ELEVEN

SPECIFIC THOUGHTS FOR TREATMENT

Symptom one: Lack of Attunement with Self

Our lack of internal and external boundaries, which results in "shape shifting" in response to the needs of those around us can leave us out-of-touch with our own needs and wants.

Addressing this fundamental lack of "self" will require us to tolerate periods of discomfort as we create time where we are left alone with ourselves. Rather than be distracted by projects, we need to spend time in "free play." We may…

- journal.

- create collages with magazines.

- take field trips to galleries or art and wine festivals where we are stimulated without a "goal" in mind.

- experiment at a mall, where we window shop to get ideas to create a living environment that supports our tastes and preferences.

- take small risks and speak with people we normally would not, just to pay attention to our own reactions and responses. Are we engaged, or do we find our mind wandering?

- listen to talk radio shows and practice forming our own opinions on the topics being discussed.

- go to a bookstore and walk through aisles we would normally skip or avoid just to see what might catch our eye.

- try new radio stations to listen to new styles of music.

- attend a cultural festival for a group you know little about, but have been curious about.

If we are the type of anxious codependent who loses ourselves, we will sometimes feel most sane when we are single. In its own all-or-nothing way, it is our experience that as soon as we begin to form a deeper bond, or merge, we will see our own hobbies, interests and focus in life begin to disappear from our calendar. We keep everything "open" in case we are needed. It will feel almost disloyal to hold onto our own lives if it in anyway may contradict or inconvenience those we love. Unfortunately, we also lose touch of our sadness and anger about giving away ourselves, so it erupts at inconvenient times, or in passive aggressive resentment behaviors. Our focus is so completely external, we no longer focus on our internal measurement of self. Those we love are given all the power to define our value and worth, and we spend so much energy monitoring our successes or failures in being what we assume others want us to be.

Developing a "self" means that we can better identify what is NOT the "self." It means that I develop an internal observer that can notice you walking towards me, and notice that my thoughts, feelings, and behaviors are different from yours. With internal boundaries, I can retain my feelings and thoughts even when yours are different, and find this curious or interesting rather than threatening.

If I can see your behavior and feelings as "information" rather than cues to my next "move," then I don't feel responsible for your thoughts and behavior. With internal boundaries I am aware that you have an entire internal life that has NOTHING to do with me, and does not require my intervention or advice or assistance. With internal boundaries I am in control of how much information I share about me, based on our level of intimacy and trust. I recognize that trust takes time. I cannot have "instant intimacy" and still be selective and self-protective. I will share with safe people and withhold from unsafe people, and internal boundaries allow me to see who is who!

External boundaries allow me to be aware that I am in control of my physical self, and that I have control over the space around me. I am in control of my possessions and I have choices about how close I get to you physically. I can choose based on my comfort zone and our level of intimacy how much time I am willing to spend with you, and whether or not I want to participate in shared activities.

Boundaries (a separate sense of "self") allow me to use my judgment to take calculated risks about how much I want to invest in relationships and activities. They will tell me when someone is pushing me somewhere I do not want to go. Boundaries allow me to disengage rather than to keep on trying to make dysfunctional situations "work." I have internal permission to make decisions based on my welfare, and not just what is "best" or most comfortable for the people around me.

How do we develop boundaries?

Internal boundaries are developed by practicing "noticing" what is happening with your body, noticing your thoughts, noticing your feelings, and noticing your behavior. Some of us may find this so difficult that we will have to keep a running notebook where once an hour we stop and write down:

- What I am feeling Physically
- What I am feeling Emotionally
- What I am Thinking
- What I am Doing

Many of us have years of practice deliberately NOT being attuned to our internal reality because we fear our needs and wants will threaten our primary relationships. Don't be surprised to find self-talk that calls you "self-indulgent," "selfish" or "foolish."

Some of us were raised by caretakers who found differences between us threatening to the relationship and saw fusion as a sign of love. They may have become angry and rejecting as we attempted to differentiate ourselves, seeing our choices as implied criticism of them as parents. It is important to invite people to participate in your life who are capable of seeing you as a separate person, even when you have a different preference. It would be great if they enjoyed the fact you have a different opinion and supported your individuality!

Maybe we tell ourselves "it doesn't matter anyway." It may well have been true that self-awareness would have caused us more misery growing up since we were powerless to change the situation. "Checking out" may have saved our sanity at one point. It is also possible once you start tuning back into yourself you may not like what you see. The difference is that you will be tuning in to yourself from a place of empowerment – you have the ability to change your situation at this point and are not at the mercy of significant attachments in your life for your survival.

Symptom Two: Lack of Attunement with Others

You may notice your behavior is intrusive at times or not considerate of those in your life. If so it is possible you operate in the world as though you are invisible because significant attachment figures did not notice your needs and wants. You learned to address them yourself without checking in with others or working cooperatively. Maybe you had to "take" what you needed regardless of the feelings of others because significant attachment figures did not respond to your needs in a timely manner or did not meet your needs appropriately.

I'll give you a painful but clear illustration of this in action.

About a month after my world disintegrated I was scheduled to visit my parents across the country because my father was ill. I was hesitant because I was in full meltdown but I promised so I went. I even told myself the break would do me good. I arrived at 11:00 pm on my birthday and my parents dutifully picked me up at the airport. I was crying in the backseat before we ever got home! At the house they had a chocolate cake for me and some presents. I cried all the way through the cake and present opening. My mom was over at the sink and my dad was at the table and no one said anything about my tears! The next day I was sitting on the couch working on the computer, crying, and my dad wandered over and asked, "How are you doing?" "Not very well, dad" I commented as snot was running down my face. "Yeah, me neither", he replied and wandered away. By the third day I was feeling psychotic, which was a perfect time for my mom and I to go to the mall. We were sitting in Subway and again I had tears running down my face. When I could no longer resist asking, "Do you not notice that I am crying?" She replied, "Yes. I figured you would talk about it if you wanted to. I didn't want to pry."

To put a positive spin on this story, you have to know that for the last month prior to my visit my friends had been checking on me daily, taking turns cooking for me, and letting me bore them with fruitless homicidal fantasies about the new "couple." So, the gift is that I saw the response I was getting from my parents as nutty instead of normal. The people who love me had given me a healthy contrast in which I was fully visible even in my craziness.

Lack of nurturing when you have been "invisible" shows up in a variety of ways. I have worked with people who would not use the bathroom for 8 hours a day at work to avoid "inconveniencing" co-workers who would have to take their position at the front desk for a short period. I have worked with people who didn't eat all day long because it was a "bother" to feed themselves. As a result we don't remember to ask others if they need to take a break when we are driving on a road trip. Or we don't think to offer a friend a sandwich or a glass of water during a visit. Rather than being self-centered it is self-abandoning though it can appear incredibly thoughtless. We don't notice when we are violating other people's boundaries because we don't have any limits on our own behavior. We are generally oblivious to the fact that we affect other people.

It is also possible that you were expected to accurately "guess" the needs and wants of your caretakers, so you never learned social skills like asking people about their preferences. This is particularly true of those raised with the "silent treatment" response. You were supposed to figure it out yourself or you would be shamed and even threatened. Consequently, you operate largely on assumptions about the needs and wants of those you love and act towards them accordingly. If this was your family pattern you will have to monitor your tendency to expect others to read your mind as well.

You will need to monitor your shame when you notice things about you that may be embarrassing or seem "immature." We have pockets of responses that are "immature" because we didn't have the secure attachment bases from which to experiment with behaviors and try out alternative responses. Instead we mastered a defense or an all-purpose response to situations because we hadn't developed awareness of the full range of available emotions, thoughts and behaviors. It is a "learning" issue not a "character" issue.

As we develop a stronger sense of self and a solid internal observer, we trust our impressions of others more, and can tune into ourselves to pick up the unspoken agendas and feelings of others. We can practice this by...

- watching movies with the sound muted to rely on language and facial expressions to follow the story line.

- "people watching" at malls, and making up storylines based on the way they carry themselves and their expressions.

- directly asking others how they feel and think about situations, and when we "think" we know, check it out by asking the other person if we are "reading them" correctly. If we are off-base, we can ask them to share more with us so we can learn better "reading others" skills.

- reading books about body language to become more familiar with physical and posture cues.

- finding someone you admire who has good attunement skills, and asking them to "coach" you.

Over time, as you practice internal observation and see yourself more accurately, you will recognize similar responses in other people, and they will seem less mysterious to you. Your ability to "tune in" to others will improve, and so will your self-esteem.

Symptom Three: Distrusting the Attachment of Others to the Codependent

This is the heart of anxious and avoidant codependence, and fuels the majority of the defenses we develop based on our "working models" about relationships. Whether we are anxious about potential abandonment, or refuse to connect to avoid the inevitable abandonment, we are often way too defended to notice or trust the stated attachment of others to us. Even when people tell us they love us and are committed to us, we are always factoring in a "Plan B." Because our efforts to shore up attachment are often founded on creating a need for us, we can never trust the attachment of others to connect to us as people. We suspect it is based on what we "do" for them, which makes failure to respond to the needs of others so dangerous. If I fail to meet your needs in a timely manner, even if it means sacrificing my own, you will simply find someone else who can do so. We always feel so expendable, and healing requires us to take risks to "be" with others without taking steps to earn their affection or attachment. This is so frightening for us – it feels vulnerable and exposed. *After all, if you had a "choice" about attaching to us, you might not make that choice.*

This means we need to find ways to be with others in "free play." We need to experiment with spending time with others in unstructured settings where connection and being in each other's company is the prime focus, and not the activity itself. We can...

- get a cup of coffee with someone, and risk sharing something personal about our thoughts, feelings or behaviors.
- invite someone to go on an errand we have been dreading, and letting the conversation and companionship make the task much easier.
- invite someone to take a drive to the ocean to simply sit and chat by the water.
- play cards or a board game with someone as an excuse to "hang out."
- offer to support someone in a task they are dreading by going along just to keep them company, not take on the task for them.
- do art projects together.

We have challenging self-talk in these areas as well, as we may be prone to filter input from others through a certain amount of paranoia – distrusting their agenda and affection for us. We need to catch ourselves testing people to see what they are "really" thinking. This kind of perspective creates an invisible barrier in relationships – it is almost impossible to be intimate with someone who is waiting for you to fail or waiting to "catch you" in a lie.

This is frequently demonstrated in the question, "Do you think that woman over there is pretty?" If he says no, he's lying. If he says yes, he would rather have sex with her than us. Maybe he is *already* having sex with her. We'll have to break into his email later and find out.

How about, "What do you love about me, honey?" Regardless of his response we can take note of all the characteristics he does not mention, creating new paranoia when encountering people who DO have those characteristics.

We can also measure their love by whether they remember our birthday or anniversary, and whether it is a large enough response if they do. We can compound our insanity by comparing the response to *other couples*, and then point this out to our partner when we are inevitably disappointed.

In all cases, the lie is, "See, I knew you were full of shit when you said you loved me." While it is painful to prove that they don't love us, **it does remove the anxiety of not being sure or waiting for abandonment**. When learning about ourselves with a therapist, we need to be honest about our own motives in our behaviors toward others. It requires "rigorous honesty" and willingness to apologize if we set someone up.

We also need to check our motives when we find ourselves volunteering to do tasks for others. Are we getting busy in order to distract ourselves from our anxiety about the "truth" of others' attachment to us. Monitoring our thoughts, feelings, bodies and behavioral cues can give us insight into our motives.

During the break-up of my business partnership, my friend was kind enough to come and sit with me as I sorted through the mounds of paper in my office. I was preparing for the move to a much smaller office and the move required a major purge. As the tears and snot smeared down my face, I was struck by how prolific I had been over the seven years. There were curricula, detailed program proposals, policies and procedures, researched information about funding opportunities, brochures... all in a child like effort to be "seen" and impress him enough to be loved. He had requested very little of it. Ultimately all those hours of work felt like failure to me because his attachment to me failed. That was my picture of how relationships were structured. It suddenly occurred to me that Bowlby was right, I had never updated my working model for relationships. My entire model was based on "earning" attachment and a lifetime of continued giving to maintain the attachment. In actuality what I "do" is the LEAST valuable part of me. I made every decision I made out of love and attempts to earn love. In between crying jags I began to forgive myself. I realized my partner gave up more than my professional contribution, he gave me up which was a far greater loss. I couldn't feel the truth of that realization for a long time, but at least it entered my thoughts.

Symptom Four: Escalation to Protect the Attachment

This particular symptom of anxious codependency requires skills for emotional regulation and management. We are up against our almost instinctive hyper-response to perceived threats, which is physiological as well as emotional. Our heart begins to race, our thoughts race, we get warm and physically restless. This level of anxiety is hard to tolerate and doing something – anything- can seem preferable to sitting still with this level of arousal. So... we make calls we regret, make asses of ourselves and say things we don't mean, all in an attempt to discharge a painful level of arousal that makes us feel like we are coming out of our skin. We dial the phone obsessively in an attempt to get a response or drive by their home repeatedly to monitor the cars in the driveway. This leads us to immoderate and extreme behaviors that, in retrospect, seem over-the-top even to us! Yet, at the time, it feels compulsively neces-sary – I HAVE to DO something!

The lengths to which we go to stay attached are truly hilarious. I remember working with a women's group as one woman described being on the neighbor's roof across from her boyfriend's house, with binoculars, monitoring his front window for the suspected "skank" he was seeing. I said, "So what if she was in there?"

She grinned, "I had my bat in the truck."

I said, "Of course you did! So the plan was to barge in, start swing-ing, and hope he'll think to himself, 'Oh, Yeah! She's the woman for me!' Because we all know nothing says 'I love you' like a new DV charge."

Of course we were in hysterics by this point, mostly because of the truth of that statement. In our own warped way we honestly believe a threat to our attachment to a loved one REQUIRES some kind of statement, like peeing on their leg to mark our territory. It never oc-curs to us if they aren't willing to respect our relationship we could simply walk away. One of the things a good Codependent prides herself on is that she's not a quitter, for God's sake.

Half the battle with this pattern is recognizing that no one is "mak-ing" us react this way. We are truly in control of our behaviors and have options in how to express our feelings. We have to decide not to abandon ourselves, to remain accountable for what comes out of our mouths as well as our effect on others.

One of the best therapies around to manage this reactivity is called Dialectical Behavioral Therapy (DBT). There are many books outlin-ing this approach quite well, especially those by Marsha Linehan, Ph.D. Two particular concepts relevant for our discussion here are Mindfulness and Primary/Secondary emotions.

One of the techniques DBT teaches to regulate and tolerate difficult emotions is Mindfulness. It's different than meditation in that you don't "clear" your mind. The goal is to learn to watch your thoughts as they pass through your mind without getting attached or stuck on one particular emotion or thought. The technique is designed to teach you to observe your thoughts without judgment. This leads us to the second concept, Primary/Secondary emotions.

Dr. Linehan has observed that we all have our immediate emotional response to events, such as fear or anger or excitement. However, we immediately "judge" these feelings as good or bad and proceed to have feelings about our first feeling or thought. So, my first feeling might have been sadness, but my immediate next thought is to judge this feeling, "That's a stupid thing to be sad about. Don't be such a cry baby." Then I feel shame about feeling sad. Dr. Linehan says that the true source of our misery is caused by the secondary emotion that is the result of our judgment about the primary emotion. Her premise is if we could feel the primary emotion without labeling or judging it, that feeling (and our distress) would pass more quickly.

The word "notice" is coming up a great deal, isn't it? This is based on my belief that if you cannot see something, you cannot change it. Accurate attunement to the self is crucial for emotional regulation, because it allows me to see situations as they unfold rather than feeling blind-sided by them.

Closely connected to noticing emotions is noticing your self-talk about your emotions and the world around you. Much of our emotional response is driven by our interpretation of events outside of us. For example, if my husband is running late from work and has not called this is only a FACT. I have choices about how to interpret that FACT.

"He's running late because he is avoiding me" = angry, hurt, anxious about the attachment

"He's running late because I am not important to him. Screw him!= defensive, avoidant, angry

"He's running later because it is the end of the quarter and he always has more workload at this time" = neutral emotions, compassion, not taking it personally

We choose how to interpret the FACT that he is running late. We also have the choice to check out our theory when he gets home. Instead, we will often match our emotions to our theory and act as if our theory is true. By the time he gets home we are in full emotional reactivity. We may even create a self-fulfilling prophecy as a result of directing so much negativity at him that he doesn't want to come home or stops caring about us! At which point we tell ourselves, "I knew it."

Here's a silly example of this. I rent an office in a wonderful building, and the owner is responsible for cleaning the two bathrooms in the building. Sometimes I will go into the bathroom and notice that the paper towels are overflowing in the trash can. As I sit down, I am next to the trash can and think to myself. "Dammit, the trash needs to be taken out AGAIN. Why doesn't he notice? He uses the same bathroom. I guess he just doesn't give a damn..." The turning point comes when I am leaving the bathroom and can either:

a. Solve the problem and take out the trash.

b. Bring it to his attention.

c. Do what I normally do, which is dismiss it from my thoughts as I head back to my office, until the next time I use the bathroom and the dialogue begins again. Sometimes this happens two or three times a day.

I am reminded of just how conflict avoidant some of us can be as I "endure" the same aggravation over and over again. I prefer to manage my irritation rather than solve the problem or risk upsetting the building owner. I never trust it will be a simple business exchange, instead I fear it will escalate for some mysterious reason just as conflicts seem to "jump off' as a child. In reality the building owner is a lovely man, pleasant to deal with and responsive. He's just very busy and probably oblivious to the problem. Why can't I trust this?

One of the things we can do to track our automatic negative thoughts is to keep a "thought journal." We write down our negative thoughts as we have them and then write an alternative thought or explanation next to it. Knowing we have a long history of interpreting situations through a distorted or fearful filter, we have to learn to ask ourselves, "Is there another possible explanation?"

The more we draw neutral conclusions and recognize how seldom people's thoughts and behaviors are about us, the more we begin to react accurately (both internally and externally). We will make fewer amends and apologies for "jumping to conclusions" and feel more self-respect and self-control.

One of the endearing aspects of women's Al-Anon meetings is how lethal our language is when we talk about people we supposedly love. I am amazed at how often women will describe their temptation to stab someone in the kitchen or shove them off a cliff or run them over. We always laugh in a companionable way and say, "Of course, I would never really do that." But we are certainly capable of fantasizing about it. I think this is a consequence of having so many relationships based on endurance. We don't just stay the course or hang in there, we endure. We persevere. We never quit. We even take a perverse pride in our ability to "love the unlovable."

All it takes is a kind comment and we tuck it away in our cheek like a squirrel and nibble on it for months until we get the next crumb. We are slowly diminishing, losing our voice, becoming invisible and we chalk it up to the "price of love." We are so busy focusing on what they say they are doing we ignore their actual behavior. This allows us to not hold them accountable, yet be surprised when they act like themselves.

Why are we always so surprised when they do the same thing they always do? I fell in love with a man who was on his third marriage due to serial infidelity. When he cheated on me I was shocked! I came unglued! How is this possible? We always think we will be different, that we will "earn" the loyalty and value for us that they have never demonstrated for others. I chose a man whose first wife threw him out for using computer porn. When I discovered him on Match.com, I was outraged! Why?

Symptom Five: Denial of Dependency or Attachment Needs

Both anxious and avoidant codependents deny their dependency needs to prepare for the eventual broken attachment. Bowlby points out that a characteristic of secure attachment is the ability to run back to our primary attachment figures for reassurance and comfort and receive consistent responses. Because we do not trust our attachments, we try not to ever put ourselves in the position of "needing" a secure-based response from someone else. We are terrified of the feelings that accompany abandonment and have a variety of defenses erected to protect us from that kind of pain.

This doesn't mean codependents don't get attached or love, it simply means we are vigilant for the possibilities (if not inevitability) that the attachment will not be there to support us when we most need it. There may well come a time when our attachment figures will decide that our needs and wants are "too much" and withdraw their willingness to provide a secure base from which to operate. Therefore we need to always hold something back in reserve, much like a secret bank account, "just in case."

It reminds me of the saying, "If you don't hope for anything you won't be disappointed." We know others are "human," which means they will always choose their best interests over ours. We keep our expectations of others fairly low. Ultimately, we believe we are the only ones who will look out for us. We call this being "realistic."

God forbid we allow ourselves to admit any need or dependency on someone. We will...

- have sex with you.
- take care of you.
- let you move into our house.

We will not:

- tell you how much money we make.
- put your name on the lease.

Frequently we fantasize about how to get rid of you whenever you threaten our comfort zone. The people we love would be really uneasy if they knew how many "Plan B's" we have. Ironically, we have back-up plans because we expect THEM to leave.

Where does this fear of being trapped or needing to take hostages and trap other people come from?

Developmental theorists would say that we are connecting attachment with engulfment. If I love you, you will move into me with a U-Haul and take me over, or if I love you I have to drive my U-Haul into you and lose myself in you. **We don't have the tools to remain independent and still connected! We don't know how to share power.**

If we are a more avoidant codependent we are hyper-aware of the subtle nuances of other people's growing attachment to us. We interpret their desire to spend more time with us or share our lives as the engine of the U-Haul turning over and we begin to take evasive maneuvers. We do this by accusing them of being controlling, by being unavailable ourselves, by compartmentalizing parts of our lives so that we appear to be more available than we are... all of these are in the service of making sure we don't disappear. But it's not the other person that will take away our freedom and self – we will give it away because on the other side of every avoidant codependent is an anxious codependent. If we let our guard down and let them in, we will flip into the anxious monitoring that makes us begin to look and feel insane. The truth is: No one takes us away – We give ourselves away! The person we most fear is us!

If we are to soften this position and entertain the notion of being "dependent" enough to have expectations for others that could leave us disappointed or hurt, we need to address our emotional regulation skills. If I do not trust my ability to be resilient in the face of distress, I am certainly not going to be willing to allow the possibility.

This brings to mind another quote from Geneen Roth's text "*Women, Food, and God.*" "*I used to think that the less I showed up the less it would hurt when I lost everything. When people I loved died. When things fell apart... The belief, unconscious as it was, that I couldn't handle, couldn't tolerate, didn't have thick enough skin or a resilient enough heart to withstand what was in front of me without fragmenting.*

On the other hand, I need to allow for the possibility of happiness and security because that could also happen (even though I never seriously considered it was possible.) In some way this is the scarier outcome because then we have more to lose. If I remain in a skeptical position, reserving my expectations, then I am safe even if guarded and lonely!

Some of us make the decision to explore a spiritual source as our first attempt to allow "dependence." Others find a spiritual source way too vague and are better off experimenting with a person such as a therapist or a sponsor if they are working a Twelve Step Program. The idea is to allow ourselves to soften some of our hard edges. It requires us to take the risk of "needing" someone for support and consistent response. To see someone or something outside of ourselves as a possible "secure base." A place we can return if we get hurt or need guidance. This is such a foreign concept for some of us that it takes time to adopt. Our original attachment figure should have provided this, but may not have been available so we are inexperienced with the idea of being "nurtured." We may truly have no idea what nurturing looks like or what it entails. Essentially it means allowing someone else to unconditionally comfort us, take care of us when we are vulnerable, to treat us as though we matter. Once you start to allow this you may find you kind of like it, even if you find it slightly embarrassing.

If you are going to begin with a spiritual "secure base" you could try:

- Going on a "God" hunt. A friend of mine describes this as looking for signs of a power greater than yourself as you go through your daily activities. Notice things that are small miracles, kindnesses, or offer you comfort as they unfold throughout the day.

- Working with a spiritual counselor or a sponsor to define this spiritual power as you understand it. You may need to revise your earlier picture of "God" developed in childhood, which most likely resembles the parents you had. If you had abandoning parents it is highly likely you may have an abandoning "higher power."

- Reading spiritual books by people you see as spiritual and you respect, like Mother Teresa, Deepak Chopra, Thich Nat Hahn, or Marianne Williams.

- Making a "God box." You will write your worries down on a piece of paper and put it in the box. Look inside the box a month later and notice ways in which your worries were resolved, maybe in ways you would never have thought of!

If you are going to begin with allowing a **person** to provide a "secure base" you could try:

- Choosing a therapist and making a commitment to attend regularly. Be as honest about your emotional reality as you are capable of being. Risk calling him/her in between sessions if you get stuck.

- Working a Twelve Step program like CODA or Al-Anon and allow someone to sponsor you. Meet with them weekly to experience consistent and loving responsiveness to your issues. Allow yourself to be treated as a priority.

- Meeting up with a friend consistently to walk or have a cup of coffee. Practice expecting them to show up every time and consistently be glad to see you. Let yourself count on it.

- Allowing someone else to drive when going places or cook a meal for you when you have had a hard week.

- Calling a friend when you are feeling lonely or anxious and share what is going on with you.

- Joining a church or support group and attending consistently so that the group can get to know you and you can begin to trust that they will consistently welcome you and recognize you. Knowing you will matter to each other, your presence would be missed if you were absent, and you would miss them. Allowing yourself to matter to them without over-doing as a volunteer. Experiment with mattering because you are you.

In the first few weeks of the ending of my professional and personal relationship with my partner, I woke up every morning hoping that the nightmare would be over. Then my chest would tighten, and I would feel the impact of the losses in my life, and I would lay there praying "God help me, God help me, God help me." And God would. And I let Him. I was so fragile that all I could do was receive for the first time in my life. My friends stepped up in shifts, making sure I had somewhere to be every evening, and every weekend. One of my friends and her husband put a bed in their extra room for me to use whenever I couldn't be alone with my ruminating thoughts. I had professional colleagues step up, creating a cheerleading squad as I relocated, and suggested an open house to celebrate my new phase in life despite my grief. I had emergency visits with my therapist, which may have inconvenienced her. I sat with friends and my sponsor and struggled to untangle an enmeshment that had left me lost and unclear. I am sure I was not always easy to spend time with. And they were unfailingly kind to me. In a divinely coordinated challenge to my old working model for relationships I could not "earn" love or attachment from anyone. I could barely get through the day, so impressive program designs and the ability to be entertaining were not an option.

Symptom Six: Avoiding Intimacy

When we talk about mattering, we are entering into the intimacy territory, a tough place for anxious and avoidant codependents. If you have been working on attunement with yourself and emotional regulations skills, you will have an easier time in this area. You will know more about yourself and have more to share at an intimate level. What does intimacy mean?

It means to allow someone to see you as you are, without masks or illusions. It means that I am consistently me regardless of the situation we are in. What you see is what you get – so I am congruent emotionally, intellectually, and behaviorally. There's no pretense.

This requires us to drop the "impression management" skills we have honed all our life to manage the impression others have of us. It is very possible that we over-identify with our image, and believe our own press! We may have been living this way for so long we have no earthly idea how to be any other way. Convinced of our foundational lack of lovability, it seems way too risky to allow people to get close enough to see our humanity. Many of us have been shamed about human imperfections, having been incorrectly taught that making mistakes is terrible, shameful, and completely unacceptable. We are "supposed" to know things without having to ask or being told. Letting someone see us in our imperfection would guarantee abandonment and broken attachment - right?

The Void, for me, was a place I entered when my partner betrayed me that felt dark, formless, infinite, with no way out. I was left with myself, someone I had disconnected from completely in the time I became immersed in him. So leaving me alone with me was the same as complete abandonment initially. I had almost no way to comfort myself because I wasn't even sure what I needed. I knew I just needed the pain to stop, but was powerless to heal myself. I needed people in my life to step into The Void with me and call me, check on me, remind me that I was still here even though he was gone and that I was going to be enough.

I absolutely could not have made this transition to life again without help. I was FORCED to trust the attachments of others to me, even though I had nothing tangible to offer them in return. I was simply too broken, and too brokenhearted to be amusing, helpful, or supportive in return.

We don't die when the worst thing that could happen to us happens.

We don't die when the attachment gets broken. Sometimes we begin to live because, like Rip Van Winkle, we awake to find there is a whole other world out there moving forward while we have been in suspended animation lost in other people's lives. We may have forgotten we exist, but the universe has not lost track of us, and the world is still waiting when we emerge, even though the re-engagement is often not our choice, and we are protesting it.

Maybe we never really made a decision to live in the first place which is why we were avoiding intimacy or losing ourselves in others. We were noncommittal about our own lives, afraid to step into our own lives with full ownership and responsibility. Instead, we hid in defensive self-reliance or anxious absorption in others as a way of establishing personal value.

The Shadow

The famous psychoanalyst Carl Jung introduced the concept of "the shadow" to describe the parts of ourselves that we push away or deny because we believe them to be unacceptable. They are qualities we see in others that we hate, that irritate us, that we judge harshly. We use a great deal of energy to deny to ourselves and others that we posses these qualities, "I'm not a jealous person – I don't have a jealous bone in my body". Or "I'm never angry, I just don't understand angry people", or "I am happiest making others happy. I can't stand selfish people." Somewhere along the way we learned that having these qualities can result in abandonment and broken attachments and we are adamant that these qualities can't be true of us. If we do see them, we feel deeply ashamed, and are very afraid other people will find out they are true of us. Others knowing our "shadow" can make us very anxious.

The more of the shadow qualities that I possess, the more guarded I will be against intimacy. I will keep the door on the closet locked pretty tight. However, Jung said we do this in vain, because these qualities will leak out of our unconscious. Debbie Ford, in her documentary on "The Shadow Effect" uses a beach ball analogy. She says to imagine trying to hold beach balls underwater in a pool. Each ball has a label like jealous, bitchy, petty, stupid. And the more balls we have, the more energy we have to exert to keep them under water.

But if we get distracted, and our attention is diverted for a moment from stuffing our beach balls, these qualities will pop out, sometimes in an embarrassing way. Such as referring to our wife as our mother, or calling someone a bitch when we never usually curse, or having an affair when we judge others very harshly who have affairs.

Carl Jung pointed out that the path to healing this was to accept all aspects of ourselves, the "good" and "bad" instead of attempting to compartmentalize and discard aspects of ourselves. These aspects are all part of being human and if we can acknowledge them, we will be more in control of their presence in our lives. For example, if I can acknowledge my capacity for jealousy, it means that instead of using my normal avoidant/dismissive attachment defenses, I will protest when our attachment is being threatened. I will be vulnerable enough to let you know I am threatened and that I need reassurance.

You may want to take some time and try this exercise.

A. List 10 qualities about you that you consider to be negative. Now, next to each write a positive use of that quality. For example:

Stubbornness	This can be helpful because it helps me stay committed to my recovery.
Anger	This can be helpful because it gives me energy to change things that make me unhappy.

B. List 10 qualities about you that you consider positive. Now next to each write a negative aspect to that quality. For example:

Patience	This can be a problem if I do not set limits when it would be in my best interest to do so.
Generous	This can be a problem because I will give things to people that they should earn themselves, so they appreciate them more.

Once we are more comfortable with the various aspects of ourselves we will have less to hide from others as well as our self. It will feel less risky to be intimate because we are able to see ourselves more realistically and with more balance. We are more likely to tell the emotional truth, and worry less about being judged. There is a lot of freedom in this.

In his book, *7 Levels of Intimacy* (92), author Matthew Kelly defines intimacy as happening when there is a mutual revealing of our authentic selves. Sometimes this is referred to as "in-to-me-see." His premise is that different kinds of communication create different levels of intimacy, and outlines 7 different levels:

1. **Clichés** - Clichés are simple conversation starters such as, "Hello, how are you?" When these are handled with ease and grace, safety is generated and people are willing to go to the next level. If they feel judged, criticized or ridiculed they will go no further. People start here to see if it is safe to connect.

   a. How are you?

   b. What have you been up to lately?

2. **Facts** - Facts can be personal or non-personal facts about the weather, sports, current events; whatever can be addressed in conversation without too much risk. Except in the case of know-it-alls, this is a great level for people to test whether a person is a safe conversationalist.

   a. Non-personal
      i. What was the score of the game?
      ii. What is the weather forecast?

   b. Personal
      i. What did you do today?
      ii. What have you learned recently?
      iii. What have you been reading lately?

3. **Opinions** - The opinion level is the first level of vulnerability, marked by a person's willingness to risk revealing something about who they are. This is often the level where conversations break down; where disagreements of opinion reveal inflexibility and intolerance. Conversely, if a person is willing to allow others to disagree without rejecting, ridiculing

or punishing, the conversation can continue to the next level.

    a. What are your preferences concerning…?

    b. What are your beliefs about…?

    c. What do you think about…?

4. **Hopes & Dreams** - If we navigate safely through the level of opinions, people will often be willing to reveal what truly inspires them. Sharing hopes and dreams identifies what a person wants to become or how they want to live. Being safe enough to entrust others with your dreams prepares you to connect at an even deeper level.

    a. If you could live any way you liked, how would you like to live?

    b. If you could live anywhere in the world, where would you like to live?

    c. What goals do you have for your life?

5. **Feelings** - When the environment is safe enough to be honest with our feelings, only then are we able to feel truly connected. Inviting someone else into our feelings, however, makes us feel vulnerable, and for most people is a difficult obstacle to overcome, depending on how accepting and validating their past experiences have been while sharing feelings with others.

    a. When in our life have you felt special to others?

    b. Who in your life made you feel safe, loved, accepted? How did they do that?

    c. Who in your life made you feel the most rejected, devalued, abandoned, invisible?

    d. What are you most passionate about?

6. **Fears** - Failures and Weaknesses - This level is uncomfortable for many of us because in our culture weakness is seen as a fault, and past sharing of one's fears and failures may have been met with ridicule and rejection rather than acceptance

and support. Conversely when openness on this level is met with care and nurturing, real healing and growth can occur.

    a. What makes you feel like you don't measure up?

    b. What makes you feel like you are unlovable?

    c. What do you think would make others reject you?

7. **Needs** - Sharing our needs in a way that is vulnerable (not demanding) is a sign of maturity, as is the ability to truly listen to one another. Sometimes our conversations lack meaning because we fail to listen or fail to ask the right questions. We fail to listen because we don't know how to subjugate our own needs in order to meet the needs of others.

    a. What do you need in order to be secure?

    b. What do you need in order to be safe?

    c. What do you need in order to be significant?

    d. What do you need in order to be competent?

Keep in mind that moving through these levels takes time – trust is not instant. There are also various types of relationships, of sharing your needs and fears may be inappropriate.

In general relationships exist at various levels:

Acquaintance – The co-worker you know by name only, or the neighbor you wave to in the morning. Cliché level primarily, maybe some facts exchanged.

Companion – This is someone with whom we share a mutual activity or interest, which is the basis of the relationship. So, the activity is primary, and getting together is simply a result of the shared interest. This is my "walking buddy" or "scrapbooking buddy". This relationship might move from cliché to facts to the opinion level.

Friendship – The basis of the relationship at this point is spending time together, and the activity becomes secondary. So, if I want to bowl and you don't, I ask you what you DO want to do, because the goal is to spend time with you. Now we're adding deeper levels, such as the hopes and dreams, feelings and fears level. In truly intimate relationship we will add our needs, because we trust the attachment well enough to know that our needs matter.

Lover – In an exclusive sexual relationship, we add sexuality to friendship and companionship to deepen our connection with the other. There is a level of intimacy that sexuality offers that marks the relationship as separate from other friendships, and our vulnerability is increased as the consequences of rejection are higher. We are completely exposed when naked, and we are declaring a boundary around our sexuality.

Commitment – This creates a boundary around our relationship as a whole, which means there is information, dependency, revealing of a depth of needs and fears that is contained within the safety of this relationship.

It is obvious that we can have any one of these relationships with varying degrees of intimacy. There are married couples who exchange cliché, factual and opinion information only. There are companions who share sex as the mutual activity. There are lovers who do not fully commit. What I have described is the path to deepening relationships so that we can gauge the intimacy expectations at each level. Let's take a look at what interferes with our ability to shift boundaries as trust begins to develop.

Symptom Seven: Walls Instead of Boundaries

We have to learn the difference between walls and boundaries. Pia Mellody points out that boundaries serve two primary functions: *Protecting us from the intrusion of others,* and *Containing our intrusive behaviors.* When we looked at lack of attunement with others, it seemed clear that our obliviousness to our impact on other people could lead us to offend them or invade their internal or external boundaries without knowing it. We could tell them how they "should" feel, because their fear or anger makes US anxious or uncomfortable. We could do their laundry to "help" without asking if they would be okay with us sorting through their personal items. We could allow similar behavior from others because of our lack of attunement with ourselves, so we would not recognize that we are uncomfortable until later, and then we may not connect our anxiety with the earlier boundary invasion. One of the goals of therapy is to feel our feelings in "real time" without this delayed reaction phenomenon. The sooner I recognize what is going on inside of me the sooner I can take care of myself or the situation.

When I do not trust my ability to make good judgments, or trust my ability to accurately be attuned to myself and others, I HAVE to have walls to protect me.

We don't need walls because other people aren't safe. We need them because we can't tell the difference between the good guys and the bad guys, and so keep everyone out just to be sure.

Lack of attunement with other's agendas, needs and feelings can make the world around us seem very confusing. We will often say, "I just don't play politics," or "I just tell it like it is. If you don't want to hear 'the truth' then don't ask me." Because we don't understand others, we will often take a position where we don't even try to connect or be tactful. We give ourselves permission to just barrel though situations, with a "take me or leave me" perspective that gives others very little room to maneuver or compromise with us. It's almost as though we expect others to work hard to get through our walls to prove they really love us. This is a lot to ask of other people.

The key to healing this aspect of our codependency will be to identify the various strategies we use to create intimacy barriers in our relationships with others. This can be challenging because we have been using these strategies for so long that we have come to believe that "this is the way I am" – we don't see them as behaviors but see them as our character.

Due to the long-term presence of these walls, we may need to solicit outside input to see ourselves accurately. We can ask people we trust to give us feedback about their first impressions of us. We can ask family members to point out our walls when they go up, and be open to the feedback even if it is uncomfortable. Remember that you cannot change behavior that you cannot see.

How to establish healthy boundaries

In order to establish healthy boundaries between yourself and others, you need to:

First: Identify the symptoms of your boundaries currently being or having been violated or ignored.

Second: Identify the irrational or unhealthy thinking and beliefs by which you allow your boundaries to be ignored or violated (e.g. It's not important, or I'm just whining).

Third: Identify new, more rational, healthy thinking and beliefs which will encourage you to change your behaviors so that you build healthy boundaries between you and others (e.g. I have a right to respectfully express a concern even if it makes someone else uncomfortable).

Fourth: Identify new behaviors you need to add to your healthy boundary skills in order to sustain healthy boundaries between you and others (e.g. Not returning phone calls when I am tired or in conversation with someone).

Fifth: Implement the healthy boundary building beliefs and behaviors in your life so that your space, privacy and rights are no longer ignored or violated. (e.g. Paying attention to my emotional and physical responses 'using my internal observer' to guide my responses with others).

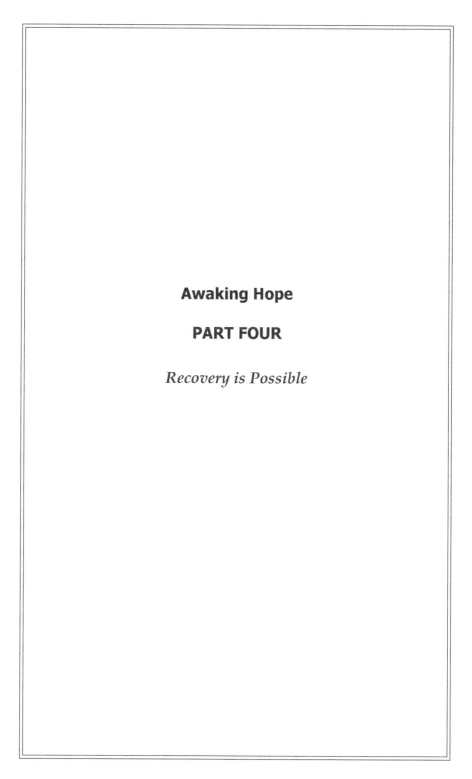

Awaking Hope

PART FOUR

Recovery is Possible

The world

Ancient

Mysterious

Undiscovered and uncharted

Mine

Chapter Twelve

Mind-Body Healing for Codependency

The mind-body connection is tightly coupled with your physical health. The implications of mind-body work are vast. Here we will focus on several key aspects:

(1) Developmental Issues
Increasing your trust in the attachment to self and others, decreasing your sense of personal vulnerability, and increasing your willingness to recognize, ask for and accept support.

Treating and resolving issues arising from early abuse or neglect will ameliorate physical problems. Examining and reforming your working models for relationships is key. This means being as honest with yourself as possible, even when it is hard.

(2) Behavioral Responses
Strengthen your Internal Observer to increase attunement with yourself and others. Notice defense mechanisms that are used to manage anxiety. Increase your ability to regulate your emotions through recognizing, acknowledging and expressing them. Decrease your reliance on substances or compulsive behaviors to artificially soothe, distract or excite internal states.

(3) Biological Consequences
Increase your ability to consciously relax, this helps to reverse the habituated stress (fight or flight) response. Increase your sensitivity to bodily needs and implement the self-care and self-protection needed to be physically healthy. Treat neglected medical symptoms and conditions that you have not "bothered" to address. Create opportunities for your body to experience regular movement in some form. Provide your body the nutrition it needs to function well. Create a sleep hygiene program that supports solid, regular sleep.

Creating a Treatment Plan

Everyone has a different combination of developmental, behavioral and biological symptoms requiring attention. I will share my plan as a general outline to get you started. Treatment plans for healing must be updated regularly. They are always a work in progress.

Developmental Issues:

Meet with a therapist weekly to examine the relational models I developed in early childhood. Look for significant working model patterns that have appeared throughout my life and begin to recognize my role in creating those patterns or being drawn into the patterns of the other person. Create new, updated working models of relationships that will support my ongoing recovery and happiness. Practice these models regularly!

Behavioral Issues:

Identify the defensive behaviors I have adopted in response to my outdated working models of relationships, for example: "earning" attachment, anticipating eventual break-up to justify not fully "anteing up" and using walls instead of boundaries. Allow care and support from friends, Al-Anon, my sponsor and others. Acknowledge personal limitations and ask for help. Practice increased emotional regulation skills and make healthy self-soothing choices. Treat myself like I matter, because I do! Continue spiritual practice through my Twelve Step Program to remind myself that I am not alone in the universe. I am loved and valued. I don't always have to have the answers.

Biological Issues:

Practice regular bed-times. Allow myself to rest when I need it instead of drinking more caffeine or eating something. Get a massage once a month, a pedicure twice a month and go to the grocery store every week to avoid eating at 7-Eleven. Re-join the aqua aerobics class I have been paying for at the YMCA for a year because it is the only exercise I can tolerate!

Spend time laying on the couch with the cats, allowing their purring to comfort me and reduce my heart-rate. Get my teeth cleaned every six months, and a physical once a year.

Allow people to hug me – a lot!

I would encourage you to spend some time creating a plan for yourself, even if you start out with just one thing on each line. Spending the time to parent yourself from a compassionate place is part of the healing process.

Developmental Issues:

_____

_____

_____

_____

_____

_____

_____

Behavioral Issues:

_____

_____

_____

_____

_____

_____

_____

Biological Issues:

_____

_____

_____

_____

_____

_____

_____

Codependency Relapse Warning Signs

After using your Treatment plan for a while and making progress in taking care of yourself, you may find yourself slipping back into old behaviors. Changing relationship patterns is incredibly hard because we are presented with opportunities to do old behaviors all day long – it is easier to stay sober by not going into a bar than to stay sane by never coming into in contact with other people!

Relapse Opportunity

My first genuine relapse challenge came four months into our separation. I was walking my client out of the building at 8:00 pm when we discovered a pile of boxes and wall hangings next to the door. My former partner had dumped every personal item I ever gave him (over the seven years) into boxes and left them in the parking lot. Every personal memento, every item from my world travels, each wall hanging, etc... The boxes were labeled, "Property of Mary Cook." My client heard me say "Oh my God" as I burst into tears. I was inconsolable in the face of such a painful dismissal. I was horrified to be sobbing in front of a client. What was I going to do with all of the items? Mostly, I felt sucker-punched. I flashed back to the Fall when I was keening and rocking on my office floor.

The scab which had started to form over my heart was ripped off without warning – in front of an audience.

The relapse risk at this point was to become overwhelmed by shame, interpreting the "dumping" of my contribution to his life as a reinforcement of my overall unloveability and lack of value. And truthfully, I did feel this way initially. And then there was the greater risk of reinforcing my distrust of attachment given how much I had once loved him.

Now for the grace of the moment:

Fortunately, this client happened to be a therapist herself and we had a long-term therapeutic relationship. She immediately understood the situation and was able to respond with compassion for me as well as take care of herself. Rather than beat myself up for being so upset, *I trusted the attachment!*

The client had just purchased a truck and promptly offered to haul the items away. We loaded the truck and she simply hauled everything away. I did not have the ability to manage the items at that point and it was far less emotional for her. *I was willing to receive help.*

I called my girlfriend and, after calming down, drove to her home. I cried some more and allowed her to comfort me. We had tea and I slept at her house. I felt less alone and I also felt loved and valued. Rather than worry about being a burden *I trusted the attachment.*

I called the building owner in the morning and made arrangements to ban my former partner from the building and property. Fortunately the building owner is an attorney with an office on site, so this was an easy task. Rather than worry about embarrassment *I trusted the attachment.*

I contacted the client the next morning to check in, offer her a free session to process her experience and thanked her again for her kindness to me the night before. I felt blessed she was there. *I experienced gratitude in the midst of pain, giving the situation balance.*

I was "restored to sanity" in under 24 hours because I was able to use the resources and support I had developed over the last four months. The attachments I had trusted were solid and secure ones.

A more general pattern:

If we are going to learn from history rather than repeat it, we have to be aware of returning to old behaviors. There are a few universal signs which indicate our attachment issues have been triggered. Most of these indicators will flare when we attempt to form an intimate attachment with someone who has difficulty forming attachments, or attaching to us consistently.

Karen is 34 years old and completing her second residential treatment for her addiction to methamphetamine. Karen remembers always feeling kind of "out there" or on her own because her family seemed to go from one crisis to another, leaving Karen to figure out how to get what she needed on her own. Even when her parents were available she was afraid to ask for something because it might "start a problem," so she developed most of her attachments to people outside the family. Unfortunately she found herself drawn to people who struggled in life. She often fell in love with men who never seemed to get a break. They always had some hurdle they were facing. Since her childhood made her so smart and resourceful she often made them feel less afraid, which made her feel useful and needed. No matter how much she tried to help them get stable they usually wound up either getting arrested or finding someone else and dumping her. When the relationships ended she always blamed herself and then began a cycle that may be familiar to you.

She would:

- Start focusing on WHY he/she isn't consistent, rather than seeing the inconsistency and choosing to not get intimately involved.

- Ruminate on WHY he/she won't commit, and see them as withholding love versus unable to form secure attachments.

- Begin to place the blame for his/her inability to attach on her unattractiveness or lack of intelligence or undesirability.

- Search for ways to make herself more desirable to EARN his/her attachment, which will likely include self-neglect in favor of expending time, energy and money to secure the attachment.

- Become willing to accept small signs of attachment from him/her rather than face the void that will open if she acknowledges their lack of full attachment.

- Act out in jealousy, control or manipulation against anyone or anything that threatens the already unstable attachment.

- Start using food, drugs, alcohol, work and other compulsive behaviors to manage her painful levels of anxiety.

- Exhibit frantic and manipulative behaviors designed to get his/her attention in an effort to connect with them and reassure herself that they are still "there" for her.

- Make excuses for his/her unavailability, using denial to protect her from the full reality of their lack of attachment.

- Obsess about their unwillingness to consistently attach to her despite her efforts to secure the attachment, and ultimately spiraling into depression and self-loathing because they won't "choose me."

- Experience sleep disturbance, stomach or chest pain, muscle aches, tension headaches, migraines, fatigue or signs that her immune system is impaired.

It may be helpful to create a list of warning signs for yourself as cues that your self-care is slipping or that you need more support. I have provided universal signs. You have your own signs you will want to list (e.g. I stop grocery shopping and go more often to drive-through).

_____

_____

_____

_____

_____

_____

Bowing in gratitude

Recipient of grace

Saved by a love

Older than time

Chapter Thirteen

Afterword

I remember early on thinking that the pain was so wrenching I would never be able to stand it. I pictured myself becoming so debilitated and catatonic that I would no longer function in any productive capacity. I remember being curled up on the therapist's couch terrified that I would never stop crying and my only hope was that I would die. I felt broken in a thousand pieces and was sure that everyone who looked at me could see my brokenness. I had not been "chosen," and the unloveability I had always "known" was real had been validated in a public and painful way. I didn't just feel broken, I was broken.

Despite this, I managed to get dressed every day, though I admit I wore a lot of black and always the same shoes. I put on make-up (though it was usually cried off by mid-day). I drove to work even though I would miss my exit half the time and had to turn around. I lost my keys and then I found them. I lost my rings and then I found them. I managed to remember to pay my rent, though I was overdrawn more than once. Somehow I crept and crawled my way back to becoming a whole person without him.

One of the supports I had during this horrendous period of time which I found incredibly comforting was the staff at Jack-in-the-Box. I was too scattered to grocery shop during this time and lived for a few months primarily on drive-through. I started every morning going through the Jack-in-the-Box by my home,

"How can I help you?"

"I'll have a breakfast steak burrito and a large iced coffee please"

"Oh, okay. No sauce, right?"

"That's right!"

"That'll be $5.79 at the window"

As I get to the window they will smile and say, "Good morning, Miss. Have a good day, we'll see you tomorrow." Sometimes the other window person would wave in the background.

I would go through a similar dialogue at the one by my office for meals later in the day. They would comment if I hadn't come by. I became part of their routine also. Honestly, I referred to them as part of my support group and found their recognition of me profoundly comforting, like the teriyaki chicken bowl, a dietary staple of mine for months.

I was touched and surprised by the cast of characters that showed up during this time in my life who were patient with me. Some of whom had no idea how important they were to me in their predictability. Like the Jack-in-the-Box guys. Like the couple who own the MailMart by my house. Like the core members of the Al-Anon groups I was attending who faithfully took their chairs every week because just seeing them made things seem "level" for an hour.

I began to remember who I was before him, and places I wanted to go and the person I wanted to be - and never was – while I was with him. There was a me before there was a him. As I re-discovered my sewing machine and returned to old beadwork tapestries I had abandoned, I remembered that I liked me. I re-discovered that I enjoy my company and I take great pleasure in watching my various "nerdy" teaching videos and mystery series. I remembered that I am hilarious and when I am fully awake I see and appreciate how ridiculous situations are. Mostly I enjoy how ridiculous I am.

I bought a new bed, something I had meant to do for years. That way all three cats could sleep with me at the same time. I traveled more, used Skype more to see the people I love around the world, took on new projects that challenged me and discovered how to use YouTube in the classroom. I reached out to people more often and more deeply appreciated how kind people can be if you give them a chance. I was more real with my godchildren who are older now. I let them see the whole of my journey from broken to healing, demonstrating that it is human nature to be resilient. Healing is part of nature, which makes taking risks a better bet. I also contacted my old counseling group partners who agreed to relocate to my new office building with me and re-establish my work as a safe environment.

I wrote a workbook to go with this text and shared it with women in recovery. I was able to see how lessons learned from my personal hell could be used for healing others. Together we laughed (and cried) over where our relationship beliefs and choices had taken us. And we kindled hope that the ending of our story is still being written – it is not destined.

On the whole I have no regrets. Being separated from the man I loved after losing so much time and money seemed like an insurmountable loss. However, I was reminded time and time again that I had retained the single most valuable thing – me. As long as I have me I can always rebuild, rebound and start over. Without me, all the energy I was expending amounted to nothing in the end. I lost everything I worked for anyway and was right back where I started, except for one important thing. Going forward I now have a new picture, a new working model for relationships in the future. I now realize as long as I choose me I can always walk away. Rather than creating a wall, this knowledge actually makes me braver and more willing to risk intimacy which is not what I would have predicted in the beginning.

The spiritual opportunity in having my heart ripped apart without anesthesia is not just surviving it but growing from it. I have a whole new perspective about what is and is not possible – what I can and cannot "stand."

When I heard how quickly he married her after we separated I rebounded pretty quickly and with minimal homicidal ideation.

That is why I dedicated the original version of this book to her – the catalyst that launched me into a void that was necessary for me to return to who I am, and always was. Without the girl in the sparkly blue tube top I would still be throwing endless and pointless energy at my partner in hopes of securing an attachment that was never sustainable.

I appreciate your willingness to accompany me on my journey out of the darkest place I have ever been. While this is designed to be a helpful text, it is also deeply personal and vital to my restoration of sanity. Thank you for taking the time to review the origins and development of Codependency, and hopefully you have been stimulated to think about the syndrome differently than you may have before. I am hoping you have a more comprehensive overview of the importance of Codependency, and can better understand why I address it seriously and not as "fad." In my experience, unaddressed codependency can destroy the mind, body and spirit. I hope this text will help you find ways to intervene effectively with your own codependency challenges as well as those of the people you may love and work with.

Recovery is possible!

Ancient wisdom

Sifted through the ashes

Not forgotten

Ever present

APPENDIX A

Ainsworth's "Strange Situation"

The "co-founder" of attachment theory, Mary Ainsworth, expanded on Bowlby's original theory in two profound ways. First, by contributing the concept of the caregiver as a secure base from which the infant explores its environment, and second by cultivating an appreciation for the role of caregiver sensitivity in the development of attachment patterns. Ainsworth explored Bowlby's theoretical approach with a famous experimental framework. She invented the "strange situation" to measure attachment status in one-year-olds. (1) The strange situation is a 24-minute laboratory procedure that involves observing the infant in a comfortable but unfamiliar room with mother, with mother and a stranger, with the stranger, and alone across multiple 3-minute episodes. She and her students observed and classified infants' response to the mild stress of separation. Children are classified as secure when they a) show distress or protest on separation, b) actively seek the parent on reunion, c) are successfully and quickly soothed if distressed, d) then return to exploratory play. Securely attached children express negative emotion openly and balance their orientation between caregiver and environment.

Ainsworth designated two categories of insecure attachment at opposite ends of a continuum: avoidant/dismissive and anxious/ambivalent. Secure attachment falls at the midpoint between these two extremes on the continuum. (2) Insecure avoidant/dismissive children protest little on separation, treat a stranger similarly to the parent, and display little or no attachment behavior during reunion. Typically they will snub the mother by turning away as she reenters the room. They may either ignore her when she tries to engage them interactively, or they may simply hover nervously nearby. In any event the child's exploration in any event is suppressed, never returning to pre-separation levels. They downplay overt manifestations of negative emotion and orient towards the environment rather than their caregiver.

Avoidant/Dismissive attached children are presumed to have had experiences where their emotional distress was not re-stabilized by the caregiver, or they were over-stimulated through intrusive parents that are likely to be distressing.

Anxious/ambivalent attached children show separation distress and proximity-seeking on reunion, but instead of being soothed while being held they squirm and sometimes kick, cling anxiously to the mother or furiously bury themselves in her lap. One subgroup seems very angry, while another is more passive. Generally these infants do not return to play. They orient toward the caregiver rather than the environment, albeit without finding comfort. Anxious/ambivalent attached children have hyperactivated emotional display, (i.e. they under-regulate their affect) (4), impulsively heightening their expression of distress possibly in an effort to elicit the response they wish to have from the caregiver. *(These are the early hallmarks of a tendency in adults to over-emphasize or even exaggerate their distress in an attempt to be "heard" or get a response)*. There is a low threshold for threat of abandonment which is easily triggered, and the child becomes preoccupied with having contact with the caregiver, yet remains frustrated even when it is available. The child cannot be sufficiently comforted by their caretaker, which can feel to the caretaker as though "enough is never enough." This has huge implications for adult relationships creating a partner who is never able to be fully reassured or at peace regardless of the efforts of their significant other.

Follow the development of an infant assessed to be resistant and demanding and angry, and one first observes a baby who has learned to maximize the attention he/she gets from the parent regardless of whether it is positive or negative (i.e., "I'd rather be screamed at than ignored"). Over time, certainly by preschool age, the child learns to manipulate the parent by alternating dramatic angry demands with needy dependence.

This child has discovered an effective way to *keep the inattentive inconsistent parent involved*: do the opposite of what mother is doing. When mother is preoccupied and not paying attention, the child explodes in angry demands and behaviors that cannot be ignored. The mother either reacts with hostility (punishing the child) or with sympathy (rewarding the child's manipulation.) This preschooler knows what to do in either case: respond to hostility with sweetness and dependency, and respond to sympathy with anger and new demands. The two are enmeshed together in a never-ending cycle of dissatisfaction. This individual grows into an emotionally volatile adolescent and adult who seeks care, but finds only partial and temporary soothing from the contact. (5)

Both the avoidant/dismissive and the anxious/ambivalent patterns of insecure infants suppress exploratory play; their behavior represents an unfortunate compromise in which the exploration required for development is sacrificed for the sake of security. Both reflect distress at separation, and both refuse when mother returns and the solution to their problem is at hand. From the secure base perspective both infants exhibit self-defeating behavior. *As much as I struggle to be close to you and long for you to comfort me, you cannot fully comfort me because I can't tolerate the intimacy, then I blame you for failing to comfort me.*

Later, researchers Main and Solomon (6) added a fourth attachment style called disorganized-insecure attachment based upon their own research. A number of studies since that time have supported Ainsworth's attachment styles and have indicated that attachment styles also have an impact on behaviors later in life.

References:

1. Ainsworth, M. (1972). Attachment and dependency: A comparison. In J. L. Gewirtz (Ed.), Attachment and Dependency. Washington, DC: V. H. Winston and Sons.

2. Ainsworth, M. (1982). Attachment: Retrospect and prospect. In C. M. Parkes & J. Stevenson-Hinde (Eds.), The Place of Attachment in Human Behaviour. London: Routledge.

3. Slade, A. (1999). Attachment theory and research: Implications for the theory and practice of individual psychotherapy with

adults. In J. Cassidy & P. R. Shaver (Eds.), Handbook of Attachment: Theory, Research, and Clinical Applications, 575-594. New York: Guilford Press

4. Sroufe, L. A. (1996). Emotional Development: The Organization of Emotional Life in the Early Years. New York: Cambridge University Press.

5. Ibid.

6. Main, M., & Solomon, J. (1986). Discovery of an insecure-disorganized/ disoriented attachment pattern: Procedures, findings and implications for the classification of behavior. In T. B. Brazelton & M. Yogman (Eds.), Affective Development in Infancy, 95-124. Norwood, NJ: Ablex.

Appendix B

A Note to Therapists
Implications for Treatment in Therapy

Bowlby saw psychotherapy as the process of helping an individual examine and rebuild dysfunctional working models. The therapist's role is to help the client "cease being a slave to old and unconscious stereotypes and to feel, to think, and to act in new ways." (1) In addition, Bowlby recognized the opportunity for the therapist to provide a corrective experience for the client in which the therapist assists the client in developing new internal working models of attachment. We can do this by providing the secure base for attachment which frees the client to explore themselves and the cognitive distortions developed from years of operating under an unhealthy working model. By providing a place of predictable and accurate response, as well as unconditional positive regard, clients can begin to practice recognizing and operating from a strengthened internal observer. These clients are increasingly able to observe their internal reality and external behaviors without being triggered by shame or fear of abandonment.

Jeremy Holmes (2) suggests that the work of therapy involves both "story-making" and "story-breaking," helping the client to knit together the events of his/her life into a coherent meaning (story-making), and to examine the events of one's life anew in light of new insights (story-breaking). Ideally these two processes form a dialectic that results in synthesis, or psychological health.

Fraiberg (3,4) worked with infants showing severely disturbed attachment patterns and found that treatment required helping the mothers to change their attachment behaviors. In every case, she found that the stumbling blocks in the current mother-infant relationship were repetitions from the mother's past. Colin (5) describes the treatment experience:

Distresses, disturbances, and conflicts from the mother's early relationships wrote the script for her baby's life. Painful old dramas replayed themselves with a new actor in an unwelcome but familiar role. The therapists sought to disengage the children from the mothers' old conflicts. To change her caregiving behavior, the mother had to exorcise the "ghosts in the nursery." She had to change her internal working model of herself as an attachment figure. To change her internal model, she had to rediscover and relive the emotions appropriate to her own early experiences of abandonment, neglect, and/or abuse.

References:

1. Bowlby, J. (1988). A Secure Base. London: Routledge. (pg. 139).

2. Holmes, J. (1998). Defensive and creative uses of narrative in psychotherapy: An attachment perspective. In G. Roberts and J. Holmes (Eds.), Narrative in Psychotherapy and Psychiatry, 49-68. Oxford, England: Oxford University Press.

3. Fraiberg, S. (1982). Pathological defenses in infancy. Psychoanalytic Quarterly, 51, 612-634.

4. Fraiberg, S., Adelson, E., & Shapiro, V. (1975). Ghosts in the nursery: A psychoanalytic approach to the problems of impaired infant-mother relationships. Journal of the American Academy of Child Psychiatry, 14, 387-422.

5. Colin, V. L. (1996). Human Attachment. Philadelphia, PA: Temple University Press. (*pp. 200-201*).

Appendix C

Psychosocial Task Development Inventory

By Dr. Richard Boyum (118)

* Based on the work of Don Hamachek, Ph.D., Michigan State University

Below you will find an inventory that will allow you to evaluate the degree to which you have successfully developed levels of trust, autonomy, initiative, industry and identity. These inventory sheets are an adaptation of Eric Erickson's Psychosocial Developmental Tasks. They should be used to give you information that will help you find your strengths and weaknesses that help in your personal, emotional development. Each category has 10 statements. Each statement is presented in terms of its' polar opposite. This means that the strength and weakness of a characteristic are presented.

You will note at the top of each stage there is a scale from +10 to -10. You are to assign yourself a single point value on each item. First determine whether your score is above or below 0 by reading both statements. Then assign yourself a number based on your own intuitive responses.

At the end of each checklist there is an opportunity for you to total your pluses and minuses. Subtract the minus total from the plus total and determine whether your total score is negative or positive. Then read the implicit attitudes that are appropriate for your plus or minus score. By completing the inventories you can determine which developmental tasks are your strong and weak points. In addition, you may find individual characteristics that you wish to work on. You may also find things that you are much stronger in than you had previously thought. Should you have questions about these items, please feel free to discuss them with a member of the counseling center staff.

Table 1

Behavioral Expressions of a Sense of Trust and Mistrust

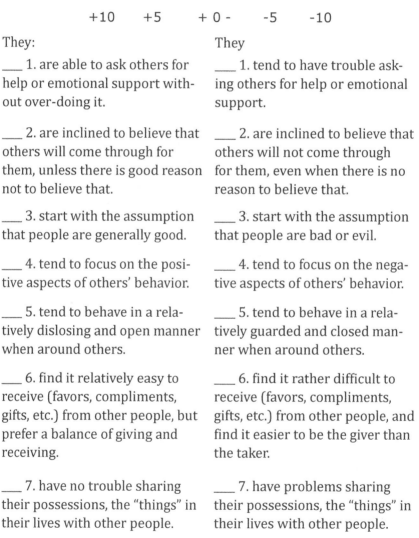

+10   +5   + 0 -   -5   -10

They:

___ 1. are able to ask others for help or emotional support without over-doing it.

___ 2. are inclined to believe that others will come through for them, unless there is good reason not to believe that.

___ 3. start with the assumption that people are generally good.

___ 4. tend to focus on the positive aspects of others' behavior.

___ 5. tend to behave in a relatively dislosing and open manner when around others.

___ 6. find it relatively easy to receive (favors, compliments, gifts, etc.) from other people, but prefer a balance of giving and receiving.

___ 7. have no trouble sharing their possessions, the "things" in their lives with other people.

They

___ 1. tend to have trouble asking others for help or emotional support.

___ 2. are inclined to believe that others will not come through for them, even when there is no reason to believe that.

___ 3. start with the assumption that people are bad or evil.

___ 4. tend to focus on the negative aspects of others' behavior.

___ 5. tend to behave in a relatively guarded and closed manner when around others.

___ 6. find it rather difficult to receive (favors, compliments, gifts, etc.) from other people, and find it easier to be the giver than the taker.

___ 7. have problems sharing their possessions, the "things" in their lives with other people.

___ 8. are not particularly fearful of disclosing themselves, even their more negative qualities, to other people.

___ 9. tend to have a generally optimistic worldview without having Pollannaish or being unrealistic about it.

___ 10. are inclined to believe that other people know what is best for themselves, even though they may privately feel differently about others choices.

Total Plus _____

Implicit Attitude:

1. You're O.K.
2. Life is generally fair and good to me.
3. I'm willing to share what I have.

___ 8. are very hesitant about disclosing themselves particularly their negative qualities, to other people.

___ 9. tend to have a generally pessimistic worldview even when things are going well and sometimes particularly when things are going well.

___ 10. are inclined to believe that other people do not know what is best for themselves, and prefer to tell others what to do.

Total Minus _____

Implicit Attitude:

1. You're not O.K.
2. Life is generally unfair and unkind to me.
3. I'm not willing to share what I have.

Table 2
Behavioral Expressions of a Sense of Autonomy and Shame and Doubt

+10   +5   + 0 -   -5   -10

They:

___ 1. like to make their own decisions, particularly about matters important to them.

___ 2. are unable to say no to requests made of them without feeling guilty.

___ 3. start with the assumption that people are generally good.

___ 4. tend to resist being dominated by people wanting to control them.

___ 5. are able to work well by themselves or with others, depending on the situation.

___ 6. are inclined to get on with what needs to be done and remain task-persistent until finished.

___ 7. can work easily with either open-ended or structured work assignments, although they may prefer more open-endedness.

___ 8. are able to listen to their own inner feelings when deciding what is right or wrong, appropriate or inappropriate .

They:

___ 1. prefer being told what to do rather than make their own decisions.

___ 2. are inclined to believe that others will not come through for them, even when there is no reason to believe that.

___ 3. are inclined to express themselves in terms of what they "should" do or "ought" to do.

___ 4. tend to allow themselves to be dominated by others, even though they may not like it.

___ 5. are not comfortable working by themselves, particularly when they know work will be judged or evaluated.

___ 6. have trouble getting started with waht needs to be done; procrastination may be a key feature of this personality.

___ 7. have problems working assignments, preferring more structure and direction.

___ 8. have difficulty listening to their own inner feelings when deciding what is right or wrong, appropriate or inappropriate.

___ 9. tend to feel relatively un-self-conscious and at ease when in group situations.

___ 9. tend to feel uneasy and self-conscious, and even em-barassed, when in group situations.

___ 10. tend to want a certain amount of order and organization in their lives to reinforce feelings of personal control and self approval.

___ 10. tend to want things "just so" as one way of avoiding others' disapproval and criticism.

Total Plus _____

Total Minus _____

Implicit Attitude:

1. I think I can do it.
2. This is what needs to be done.
3. I have something of value to offer.

Implicit Attitude:

1. I don't think I can do it.
2. Tell me what needs to be done.
3. I have little of value to offer.

Table 3
Behavioral Expressions of a Stage of Initiative and Guilt

+10   +5   + 0 -   -5   -10

They:

___ 1. prefer to get on with what needs to be done to complete the task at hand.

___ 2. like accepting new challenges now and then.

___ 3. tend to be self starters.

___ 4. tend to be effective leaders when in that position.

___ 5. tend to set goals and then set out to accomplish them.

___ 6. tend to have high energy levels.

___ 7. have a strong sense of personal adequacy.

___ 8. seem to enjoy "making things happen."

___ 9. are able to emotionally appreciate the idea that initiative begins and ends with the person, not the production it generates.

They:

___ 1. tend to postpone, put off, put aside, and generally procrastinate starting.

___ 2. are inclined to resist new challenges.

___ 3. tend to be slow self-starters.

___ 4. tend to be ineffective leaders when in that position.

___ 5. may set goals but have problems getting them accomplished.

___ 6. tend to have low energy levels.

___ 7. have a weak sense of personal adequacy.

___ 8. prefer to remain in the background, preferring not to stir things up.

___ 9. may try to outrun their guilt with a tireless show of accomplishment, believing that efficient production may compensate for being a deficient person.

___ 10. have a balanced sense of right and wrong without being overly moralistic.

___ 10. tend to focus moralistically on those things in life that are "wrong."

Total Plus _____

Total Minus _____

Implicit Attitude:

1. I will start now.

2. I enjoy new challenges.

3. This is what needs to be done and I will do it.

Implicit Attitude:

1. I will start tomorrow.

2. I prefer sticking with what I know.

3. This is what needs to be done, but who will do it?.

Table 4
Behavioral Expressions of a Sense of Industry and Inferiority

+10   +5   + 0 -   -5   -10

They:

___ 1. enjoy learning about new things and ideas.

___ 2. reflect a healthy balance between doing what they have to do and what they like to do.

___ 3. reflect strong curiosities about how and why things work the way they do.

___ 4. enjoy experimenting with new combinations, new ideas, and arriving at new syntheses.

___ 5. are excited by the idea of being producers.

___ 6. like the recognition that producing things brings, which reinforces sense of industry.

___ 7. develop a habit of work completion through steady attention and preserving diligence.

___8. have a sense of pride in doing at least one thing well.

___ 9. take criticism well and use it to improve their performance.

___ 10. end to have a strong sense of patience.

They:

___ 1. do not particularly enjoy learning about new things and ideas.

___ 2. tend to concentrate.

___ 3. are not terribly curious about how and why things work.

___ 4. prefer staying with what is known; new ways do not attract them so much as do proven ways.

___ 5. tend to be threatened, even guilty, about the idea of being producers.

___ 6. would like the recognition that production brings, but sense of inferiority stands in the way.

___ 7. develop a habit of work delay by ongoing procrastinations.

___ 8. have problems taking pride in their work, believing it is not worth it.

___ 9. take criticism poorly and use it as a reason to stop trying.

___ 10. tend to have a weak sense of persistence.

Total Plus _____   Total Minus _____

Implicit Attitude: Implicit Attitude:

1. I'm a pretty good learner   1. I'm not a very good learner.

2. Being a producer excites me. 2. Being a producer frightens me.

3. I'll work hard to succeed.   3. I'll work hard to avoid failing

Table 5
Behavioral Expressions of a Sense of Identity and Identity Confusion

+10 +5 + 0 - -5 -10

They:

___ 1. have a stable self-concept that does not easily change.

___ 2. are able to combine short-term goals with long-range plans.

___ 3. are less susceptible to the shifting whims of peer pressure influences.

___ 4. tend to have reasonably high levels of self-acceptance.

___ 5. are able to make decisions without undue wavering and indecisiveness.

___ 6. tend to be optimistic about themselves, others, and life generally.

___ 7. tend to believe that they are responsible for what happens to them, good or bad.

___ 8. are able to seek self-acceptance directly by being their own person.

___ 9. are able to be physically and emotionally close to another person without fearing a loss of self.

They:

___ 1. tend to have an unstable self-concept marked by ups and downs.

___ 2. tend to set short-term goals, but have trouble establishing long-range plans.

___ 3. are more susceptible to the shifting whims of peer pressure influences.

___ 4. tend to have rather low levels of self-acceptance.

___ 5. are apt to have trouble making decisions, fearing that they will be wrong.

___ 6. tend to have somewhat cynical attitudes about themselves, others, and life generally.

___ 7. tend to believe that what happens to them is largely out of their hands, a matter of fate or breaks.

___ 8. are inclined to seek self-acceptance indirectly by being what they believe others want them to be.

___ 9. are inclined to have trouble being physically and emotionally close to another person without being either too dependent or too separate.

___ 10. tend to be cognitively flexible; their sense of self does not depend on being "right."

___ 10. tend to be cognitively inflexible; their sense of self resides heavily on being "right."

Total Plus _____

Total Minus _____

Implicit Attitude:

1. I am this kind of person.

2. I'm not perfect, but I'm still O.K.

3. I can accept your shortcomings because I can accept my own.

Implicit Attitude:

1. I'm not a very good learner.

2. Being a producer frightens me.

3. I'll work hard to avoid failing

Table 6
Behavioral Expressions of a Sense of Intimacy and Isolation

+10   +5   + 0 -   -5   -10

They:

___ 1. have been able to establish a firm sense of their own identity.

___ 2. tend to be tolerant and accepting of the differences perceived in other people.

___ 3. are willing and able to trust others and themselves in the relationships they form.

___ 4. are able to form close emotional bonds without fearing the loss of their own identity.

___ 5. tend to develop cooperative, affiliative relationships with others.

___ 6. find satisfaction in their affiliation with others but can comfortably isolate themselves and be alone when they choose.

___ 7. are willing and able to commit themselves to relationships that demand sacrifice and compromise.

___ 8. are inclined to perceive relationships as something one gives to.

They:

___ 1. have not been able to establish a firm sense of their own identity.

___ 2. tend not to be particularly tolerant or accepting of differences perceived in other people.

___ 3. are not particularly willing to trust either themselves or others in the relationships they form.

___ 4. are hesitant to form close emotional bonds because of fear of losing self-identity.

___ 5. tend to develop competitive relationships with others, making cooperative efforts more difficult.

___ 6. tend to prefer more separation from others; they feel uncomfortable when affiliations with others are too close.

___ 7. have difficulty committing to relationships that demand sacrifice and compromise.

___ 8. are inclined to perceive relationships as something one takes from.

___ 9. tend to perceive sex as a means of both achieving physical closeness and expressing love; partner is seen as a person.

___ 9. tend to perceive sex as a means of achieving physical satisfaction but not necessarily expressing love; partner is seen more as an object.

___ 10. are able to express their caring feelings in a variety of ways and to say the words "I love you" without fear.

___ 10. have difficulty expressing their feelings for others and find the words "I love you" hard to verbalize.

Total Plus _____

Total Minus _____

Implicit Attitude:

1. I'm okay and others are too.
2. Others can generally be trusted.
3. Life can be difficult, but through mutual interdependence we can make it.

Implicit Attitude:

1. I'm okay, but others are not okay.
2. Others cannot generally be trusted.
3. 3. Life can be difficult, and people have to learn to take care of themselves.

Table 7
Behavioral Expressions of a Sense of Generativity and Stagnation

+10   +5   + 0 -   -5   -10

They:

___ 1. feel personally concerned about others, their immediate family, which includes future generations and the nature of the world in which those generations will live.

___ 2. reflect varying degrees of involvement with enhancing the welfare of young people and making the world a better place for them to live and work.

___ 3. have an interest in producing and caring for children of their own.

___ 4. reflect a parental kind of concern for the children of others.

___ 5. tend to focus more on what they can give to others rather than on what they get.

___ 6. tend to be absorbed in a variety of activities outside of themselves.

___ 7. are interested in leading productive lives and in contributing society.

___ 8. display other-centered values and attitudes.

They:

___ 1. are concerned primarily with themselves and show little interest in future generations.

___ 2. show little by way of involvement with the welfare of young people and helping to make the world a better place to live and work.

___ 3. have little interest in producing or caring for children of their own.

___ 4. show little by way of a parental kind of concern for the children of others.

___ 5. tend of focus more on what they can get from others rather than on what they can give.

___ 6. tend to be absorbed primarily in themselves and their own needs.

___ 7. are not particularly interested in being productive or in contributing to society.

___ 8. display self-centered values and attitudes.

___ 9. are interested in enhancing what is known, even if it means changing the status quo.

___ 9. are interested in maintaining and preserving what is known in order to conserve the status quo.

___ 10. feel a strong inclination to develop some unique talent or to express themselves creatively.

___ 10. do not feel any particular inclination to develop some unique talent or to express themselves creatively.

Total Plus _____

Total Minus _____

Implicit Attitude:

1. What can I give to others?
2. Risks I would like to take include.
3. I enjoy being productive and creative.

Implicit Attitude:

1. What can I get from others?
2. Risks I would like to avoid include.
3. I prefer routine and sameness.

Table 8
Behavioral Expressions of Integrity and Despair

+10   +5   + 0 -   -5   -10

They:

___ 1. reflect many of the positive ego qualities associated with earlier stages, such as trust, autonomy, initiative, industry and identity.

___ 2. believe that who they are and what they become are largely the consequences of their own choices.

___ 3. accept the idea that this is their one and only life and that what has happened to it is largely of their own doing.

___ 4. accept death as an inevitable part of the life cycle.

___ 5. are able to admit to themselves and others that, for the most part, they have no one but themselves to blame for whatever troubles or failures they have experienced.

___ 6. are ready and able to defend the dignity of their own life-styles against all physical economic threats, that is, they are not easily pushed around.

___ 7. are able to look back on their lives with feelings of pleasure, gratefulness, and appreciation.

They:

___ 1. reflect many of the negative qualities associated with earlier stages, such as mistrust, shame, guilt, inferiority, and identity confusion.

___ 2. are inclined to believe that who they are and what they have become is not something over which they have had much control.

___ 3. have trouble accepting the idea that this is their one and only life and that what has happened to it is largely their own doing.

___ 4. show signs of fearing death and do not accept it as part of the life cycle.

___ 5. tend to blame others for whatever troubles or failures they have experienced.

___ 6. offer little resistance to physical and economic threats

___ 7. tend to look back on their lives with feelings of displeasure, regret, and depreciation.

___ 8. tend to be reasonably happy, optimistic people, satisfied with their lives.

___ 9. approach the final stage of their lives with a sense of personal wholeness.

___ 10. are able to integrate their past experiences with current realities, and in this way generate a kind of "wisdom" about how to live one's life and cope successfully.

Total Plus _____

Implicit Attitude:

1. I have much to be thankful for.
2. I am in control of my life.
3. I accept myself for who I am, and I accept others for who they are.

___ 8. tend to be fairly unhappy, pessimistic people, dissatisfied with their lives.

___ 9. approach the final stage of their lives with a sense of personal fragmentation, an incompleteness.

___ 10. seem stuck at the level of blame and disappointment, which makes it difficult for them to learn from their mistakes.

Total Minus _____

Implicit Attitude:

1. I have little to be thankful for.
2. I have little control over what happens to me.
3. I do not accept myself for who I am, and I wish others could be different.

Footnotes: Developmental Section

1. Bowlby, J. (1979). The Making and Breaking of Affectional Bonds. London: Tavistock.

2. Bowlby, J. (1988). A Secure Base. London: Routledge Publishing.

3. Winnicott, D. W. (1971). Playing and Reality. London: Penguin

4. Donovan, W. L., & Leavitt, L. A. (1985). Physiological assessment of mother-infant attachment. Journal of the American Academy of Child Psychiatry, 24, 65-70.

5. Winnicott, D. W. (1971). Playing and Reality. London: Penguin

6. Greenberg, S., & Mitchell, S. (1983). Object Relations in Psychoanalytic Theory. Cambridge, MA: Harvard University Press.

7. Harris, P. L. (1994). The child's understanding of emotion: Developmental change and the family environment. Journal of Child Psychology and Psychiatry, 35, 3-28.

8. Grossmann, K. E., & Grossmann, K. (1991). Attachment quality as an organizer of emotional and behavioral responses in a longitudinal perspective. In C. M. Parkes, J. Stevenson-Hinde, & P. Marris (Eds.), Attachment Across the Life Cycle, 93-114. London: Tavistock/Routledge.

9. Reed, M. D. (1993). Sudden death and bereavement outcomes: The impact of resources on grief symptomatology and detachment. Suicide and Life Threatening Behavior, 23(3), 204-220.

10. Crittenden, P. M. (1992). Quality of attachment in the preschool years. Development and Psychopathology, 4, 209-241.

11. Crittenden, P. M. (1993). Information processing and Ainsworth's patterns of attachment. Paper presented at John Bowlby's Attachment Theory: Historical, Clinical, and Social Significance. C. M. Hinks Institute, Toronto, Canada.

12. Bowlby, J. (1973). Attachment and Loss: Vol. 2. Separation. New York: Basic Books.

13. Zimberoff, D., & Hartman, D. (2001). Four primary existential themes in Heart-Centered Therapies. Journal of Heart-Centered Therapies, 4(2), 3-64.

14. Dayton, Tian, Ph. D (2007). <u>Emotional Sobriety: From Relationship Trauma to Resilience and Balance</u>, HCI: *p. 150-151*

15. Peck, Scott. (1998) . TouchThe Road Less Traveled and Beyond: Spiritual Growth in an Age of Anxiety. Touchstone Publishers.l

16. Sroufe, L. A., & Fleeson, J. (1986). Attachment and the construction of relationships. In W. Hartup & Z. Rubin (Eds.), Relationships and Development, 51-71. Hillsdale, NJ: Erlbaum.

17. Bretherton, I., & Munholland, K. A. (1999). Internal working models in attachment relationships: A construct revisited. In J. Cassidy & P. R. Shaver (Eds.), Handbook of Attachment: Theory, Research and Clinical Applications, 89-111. (pg.91)New York: Guilford Press.

18. Caspi, A., & Elder, G. H. (1988). Emergent family patterns: The intergenerational construction of problem behavior and relationships. In R. A. Hinde & J. Stevenson-Hinde (Eds.), Relationships Within Families, 218-240. Oxford, England: Clarendon Press.

19. Bretherton, I., & Munholland, K. A. (1999). Internal working models in attachment relationships: A construct revisited. In J. Cassidy & P. R. Shaver (Eds.), Handbook of Attachment: Theory, Research and Clinical Applications, 89-111. New York: Guilford Press.

20. Bartholomew K, Horowitz LM (August 1991). "Attachment styles among young adults: a test of a four-category model". *J Pers Soc Psychol* 61 (2): 226–44. doi:10.1037/0022-3514.61.2.226. PMID 1920064. http://content.apa.org/journals/psp/61/2/226

21. Baldwin, M. W. (1992). Relational schemas and the processing of social information. Psychological Bulletin, 112, 461-484.

22. Baldwin, M. W. (1997). Relational schemas as a source of if-then self-inference procedures. Review of General Psychology, 1, 326-335.

23. Baldwin, M. W., Fehr, B., Keedian, E., Seidel, M., & Thompson, D. W. (1993). An exploration of the relational schemata underlying attachment styles: self-report and lexical decision approaches. Personality and Social Psychology Bulletin, 19, 746-754.

24. Baldwin, M. W., & Fehr, B. (1995). On the Instability of Attachment Style Ratings. Personal Relationships, 2, 247-261.

25. Baldwin, M. W., Keelan, J. P. R., Fehr, B., Enns, V., & Koh-Rangarajoo, E. (1996). Social-cognitive conceptualization of attachment working models: Availability and accessibility effects. Journal of Personality and Social Psychology, 71, 94-109.

26. Baldwin, M. W., & Meunier, J. (1999). The Cued Activation of Attachment Relational Schemas. Social Cognition, 17, 209-227.

27. Baldwin, M. W. (1992). Relational schemas and the processing of social information. Psychological Bulletin, 112, 461-484. (pg.429)

28. Bowlby, J. (1980) Loss: Sadness & Depression, in Vol. 3 of Attachment and loss, London: Hogarth Press. New York: Basic Books; Harmondsworth: Penguin (1981).

29. Bretherton, I. (1985). Attachment theory: Retrospect and prospect. Monographs of the Society for Research in Child Development, 50 (1-2, Serial No. 209).

30. Bretherton, I. (1990). Open communication and internal working

models: Their role in the development of attachment relation-ships. In R. A. Thompson (Ed.), Nebraska Symposium on Motivation, 36, 57-113. Lincoln: University of Nebraska Press.

31. Collins, N., & Read, S. J. (1994). Cognitive representations of attachment: The structure and function of working models. In D. Perlman & K. Bartholomew (Eds.), Advances in personal relationships (Vol. 5, pp. 53-90). London: Jessica Kingsley.

32. Main, M., Kaplan, K., & Cassidy, J. (1985). Security in infancy, childhood, and adulthood: A move to the level of representation. Monographs of the Society for Research in Child Development, 50 (1-2, Serial No. 209).

33. Pietromonaco, P. R., & Barrett, L. F. (2000). The internal working models concept: What do we really know about the self in relation to others? Review of General Psychology, 4, 155-175. (pg.159)

34. Trinke, S. J., & Bartholomew, K. (1997). Hierarchies of attachment relationships in young adulthood. Journal of Social and Personal Relationships, 14, 603-625.

35. La Guardia JG, Ryan RM, Couchman CE, Deci EL (September 2000). "Within-person variation in security of attachment: a self-determination theory perspective on attachment, need fulfillment, and well-being". J Pers Soc Psychol 79 (3): 367–84. doi:10.1037/0022-3514.79.3.367. PMID 10981840. http://content.apa.org/journals/psp/79/3/367.

36. Mikulincer, M., Shaver, P. R., & Pereg, D. (2003). Attachment theory and affect regulation: The dynamics, development, and cognitive consequences of attachment-related strategies. Motivation and Emotion, 27, 77-102.

37. Ibid

38. Hazan, C., & Shaver, P. R. (1990). Love and work: An attachment theoretical perspective. Journal of Personality and Social Psychology, 59(2), 270-280.

39. Salzman, L. (1979). Psychotherapy of the obsessional. American Journal of Psychotherapy, 33(1), 32-40.

40. Descutner, C. J., & Thelen, M. H. (1991). Development and validation of a Fear of Intimacy Scale. Psychological Assessment, 3(2), 218-225.

41. Lutwak, N. (1985). Fear of intimacy among college women. Adolescence, 20(77), 15-20.

42. West, M., Rose, M. S., & Sheldon, A. (1993). Anxious attachment as a determinant of adult psychopathology. Journal of Nervous and Mental Disease, 181(7), 422-427.

43. Sroufe, L. A. (1983). Infant-caregiver Attachment and Patterns of Adaptation in Preschool: The Roots of Maladaptation and Competence, Vol. 16. Hillsdale, NJ: Erlbaum.

44. Sroufe, L. A., Egeland, B., & Kreutzer, T. (1990). The fate of early experience following developmental change: Longitudinal approaches to individual adaptation in childhood. Child Development, 61, 1363-1373.

45. Ainsworth, M., Blehar, M. C., Waters, E., & Wall, S. (1978). Patterns of Attachment: A Psychological Study of the Strange Situation. Hillsdale, NJ: Lawrence Erlbaum Associates.

46. Gottman, J. M. (1993). Studying emotion in social interaction. In M. Lewis & J. Haviland (Eds.), Handbook of Emotion, 475-488. New York: Guilford Press.

47. Holmes, J. (1993). Attachment theory: A biological basis for psychotherapy? British Journal of Psychiatry, 163, 430-438.

48. Walant, K. B. (1995). Creating the Capacity for Attachment: Treating Addictions and the Alientated Self. Northvale, NJ: Jason Aronson.

49. Flores, P. J. (2001). Addiction as an attachment disorder: Implications for group therapy. International Journal of Group Psychotherapy, 51(1), 63-81.

50. Cooper, M. L., Frone, M. R., Russell, M., & Mudar, P. (1995). Drinking to regulate positive and negative emotions: A motivational model of alcohol use. Journal of Personality and Social Psychology, 69, 990-1005.

51. Ibid

52. Magai, C. (1999). Affect, imagery and attachment. In J. Cassidy & P. R. Shaver (Eds.), Handbook of Attachment: Theory, Research and Clinical Applications, 787-802. New York: Guilford Press

53. O'Connor, L. E., Berry, J. W., Inaba, D., & Weiss, J. (Nov-Dec, 1994). Shame, guilt, and depression in men and women in recovery from addiction. Journal of Substance Abuse Treatment, 11(6), 503-510.

54. Holmes, J. (1997). Attachment, autonomy, intimacy: Some clinical implications of attachment theory. British Journal of Medical Psychology, 70, 231-248. (p.233).

55. Lieberman, A. F., & Pawl, J. H. (1988). Clinical applications of attachment theory. In J. Belsky & T. Nezworski (Eds.), Clinical Applications of Attachment, 327-351. Hillsdale, NJ: Lawrence Erlbaum Associates.

56. Holmes, J. (1997). Attachment, autonomy, intimacy: Some clinical implications of attachment theory. British Journal of Medical Psychology, 70, 231-248. (p.233).

57. Mickelson, K. D., Kessler, R. C., & Shaver, P. R. (1997). Adult attachment in a nationally representative sample. Journal of Personality and Social Psychology, 73, 1092-1106.

58. Sroufe, L. A. (1996). Emotional Development: The Organization of Emotional Life in the Early Years. New York: Cambridge University Press.

59. Cole-Detke, H., & Kobak, R. (1996). Attachment processes in eating disorder and depression. Journal of Consulting and Clinical

Psychology, 64(2), 282-290.

60. Warren, S. L., Huston, L., Egeland, B., & Sroufe, A. (1997). Child and adolescent anxiety disorders and early attachment. Journal of the American Academy of Child and Adolescent Psychiatry, 36(5), 637-644.

61. Rosenstein, D., & Horowitz, H. (1996). Adolescent attachment and psychopathology. Journal of Consulting and Clinical Psychology, 64(2), 244-253.

62. Patrick, M., Hobson, R., Castle, D., Howard, R., & Maughn, B. (1994). Personality disorder and mental representation of early social experience. Development and Psychopathology, 6, 375-388.

63. Cole-Detke, H., & Kobak, R. (1996). Attachment processes in eating disorder and depression. Journal of Consulting and Clinical Psychology, 64(2), 282-290.

64. Rosenstein, D., & Horowitz, H. (1996). Adolescent attachment and psychopathology. Journal of Consulting and Clinical Psychology, 64(2), 244-253.

65. Main, M., & Morgan, H. (1996). Disorganization and disorientation in infant strange situation behavior: Phenotypic resemblance to dissociative states. In L. K. Michaelson & W. J. Ray (Eds.), Handbook of Dissociation: Theoretical, Empirical, and Clinical Perspectives, 107-138. New York: Plenum Press.

66. Ogawa, J. R., Sroufe, L. A., Weinfield, N. S., Carlson, E. A., & Egeland, B. (1997). Development and the fragmented self: Longitudinal study of dissociative symptomatology in a nonclinical sample. Development and Psychopathology,9, 855-879.

67. Winnicott, D. W. (1965). The Maturational Processes and the Facilitating Environment. New York: International Universities Press.

68. Mellody, Pia,, Miller, Andre Wells, Miller, Miller, Keith J. (1989)

Facing Codependence: What It Is, Where It Comes from, How It Sabotages Our Lives. Harper and Row.

69. Weinhold, Janae and Barry, Ph.D. (2ⁿᵈ Ed., 2008) Breaking Free of the Co-Dependency Trap. New World Library

70. Bee, Helen and Boyd, Denise. (2004). The Developing Child. (10th ed.). Boston: Pearson.

71. Alen, K. E., & Marotz, L. R. (2003). Developmental profiles (4th ed.). Albany, NY: Delmar. Bullock, J. (2002).

72. Ibid

73. Childhood and Society: By Erik H. Erikson. New York: W. W. Norton & Co., Inc., 1950. pp.397

74. Maunder, R. G., & Hunter, J. J. (2001). Attachment and psychosomatic medicine: Developmental contributions to stress and disease. Psychosomatic Medicine, 63(4), 556-567. p. 556.

75. Lachlan A. McWilliams, PhD, and S. Jeffrey Bailey, PhD "Associations Between Adult Attachment Ratings and Health Conditions: Evidence From the National Comorbidity Survey Replication," Acadia University; *Health Psychology*, Vol. 29, No.

76. Stuart, S., & Noyes, R. (1999). Attachment and interpersonal communication in somatization. Psychosomatics, 40, 34-43.

77. Sroufe, L. A., & Waters, E. (1977). Heart rate as a convergent measure in clinical and developmental research. Merrill-Palmer Quarterly, 23, 3-27.

78. Florian, V., & Mikulincer, M. (1995). Effects of adult attachment style on the perception and search for social support. Journal of Psychology, 129, 665-676.

79. Mikulincer, M., & Florian, V. (1995). Appraisal of and coping with a real-life stressful situation: The contribution of attachment styles. Personality and Social Psychology Bulletin, 21,

406-414.

80. Ognibene, T. C., & Collins, N. L. (1998). Adult attachment styles, perceived social support, and coping strategies. Journal of Social and Personal Relationships, 15, 323-345.

81. Simpson, J. A., Rholes, W. S., & Nelligan, J. S. (1992). Support seeking and support giving within couples in an anxiety-provoking situation: The role of attachment styles. Journal of Personality & Social Psychology, 62, 434-446.

82. House, J. S., Landis, K. R., & Umberson, D. (1988). Social relationships and health. Science, 241, 540-545.

83. Kobak, R., & Sceery, A. (1988). Attachment in late adolescence: Working models, affect regulation, and representation of self and others. Child Development, 59, 135-146.

84. Mikulincer, M. (1999). Adult attachment style and affect regulation: Strategic variation in self-appraisals. Journal of Personality and Social Psychology, 75, 420-435.

85. Magai, C. (1999). Affect, imagery and attachment. In J. Cassidy & P. R. Shaver (Eds.), Handbook of Attachment: Theory, Research and Clinical Applications, 787-802. New York: Guilford Press.

86. Raynes, E., Auerbach, C., & Botyanski, N. C. (1989). Level of object representation and psychic structure deficit in obese persons. Psychological Reports, 64, 291-294.

87. Feeney, J. A., & Raphael, B. (1992). Adult attachments and sexuality: Implications for understanding risk behaviours for HIV infection. Australia and New Zealand Journal of Psychiatry, 26, 399-407.

88. Kotler, T., Buzwell, S., Romeo, Y., & Bowland, J. (1994). Avoidant attachment as a risk factor for health. British Journal of Medical Psychology, 67, 237-245.

89. Ciechanowski, P., Dwight, M., Katon, W., & Rivera-Ball, D. (1998). Attachment classification associated with unexplained medical symptoms in patients with chronic hepatitis C. Proceedings of the Second International Attachment and Psychopathology Conference, Toronto, Canada.

90. Felitti, V. J., Anda, R. F., Nordenberg, D., Williamson, D. F., Spitz, A. M., Edwards, V., Koss, M. P., & Marks, J. S. (1998). Relationship of childhood abuse and household dysfunction to many of the leading causes of death in adults: The Adverse Childhood Experiences (ACE) Study. American Journal of Preventive Medicine, 14(4), 245-58.

91. Weinhold, Janae and Barry, Ph.D. (2nd Ed., 2008) Breaking Free of the Co-Dependency Trap. New World Library

92. http://www.selfcounseling.com/help/personalsuccess/taskdevelopment.html.

If you wish to contact Mary please feel free to call, send an email, or a letter.

Mary Crocker Cook

1710 Hamilton Ave. #8

San Jose, CA 95125.

Phone: (408) 448-0333

Email: marycook@connectionscounselingassociates.com

For more information about Mary's counseling services or presentation topics visit:

www.marycrockercook.com

CPSIA information can be obtained at www.ICGtesting.com
Printed in the USA
BVOW102041250313

316403BV00006B/95/P